Diving into Sunsets:
A Physician's Memoir of
His Dying Dog and Dad

David M. Liscow, MD

Copyright © 2013
Digibuzz Multimedia, LLC
All rights reserved.
ISBN: 0615736610
ISBN-13: 9780615736617

For all those who remain after the sun sets

CONTENTS

Acknowledgements

Why My Dog and Dad   pg. 1

Of Human Canine Bonds
or My Living Bond with My Dying Dog   pg. 7

Epilogue   pg. 160

A Father's Last Hours with His Physician Son   pg. 166

The Eulogy   pg. 214

Afterword   pg. 218

ACKNOWLEDGMENTS

I wish to express my deepest gratitude, first and foremost, to my wife who has partnered with me in bringing this book to press and in all aspects of my life. I would also like to thank Izzy's Veterinarian, Lisa Bucht, DVM, whose skill and care allowed me to have this incredible island of time with our dying dog. Along the same lines, I would like to thank all those patients and colleagues who shared their experiences and gave me their ears, making it easier for me to bear the unknown at the end. "Deer Candy", you are in this group. I would also like to thank my Cincinnati family who really took care of my father's needs during the final months of his life (while I lived and worked in Michigan) and allowed me to have the role I had at the end. Finally, I would like to thank my two sons who put up with the most annoying dog in the neighborhood during their formative years and allowed their parents to experience the noble behavior of his sunset.

WHY MY DOG AND DAD

The two companion pieces that comprise this book, Diving into Sunsets, were written during the year 2006 after the departure of two important presences in my life. My father died January 15th, less than a month after his 78th birthday, and my dog died a Friday October 13th, a few months before his 13th birthday, or at the age of 81 in large-dog years. Both pieces were conceived by a union of pain and unexpected joy, and both had to be written as one must sleep after a long period of exhausting labor, eat after a day of fasting, or love after an extended period of abstinence. Once written, though at times personal in nature, I believed that my experience as a family physician which included assisting patients in the birthing process, guiding them through their final weeks and days, and everything between, offered an uncommon perspective on common experiences. I also believed that while the pieces contained much of what is common in the human experience, they attempted to express what is often left unsaid. When they were in a nearly complete form, I stashed them away, waiting for the day when it would be possible to share them with a larger audience.

The pieces may seem odd bedfellows in a single book. The first was written while I was still in the turbulent flow of the aftermath of the death of a human being, not just any human being, my father. I wrote it because I found the event almost transcendent, a culmination of who I was personally and professionally on one level, and an experience profoundly spiritual and mystical on another. I was able to fulfill what might have been one of my father's dying wishes—I tended to his medical care during the last hours of his life and remained his loving son at the same time, roles not always compatible. But once my father had taken his last breath, I experienced a sublimity and serenity that completely surprised me, not unlike what new parents experience after a tumultuous labor, when peace finally reigns and the parents gaze into the long-awaited face and explore the tiny hands of their newborn child. All my siblings experienced it; not just me. This was one of the more important experiences that had to be told.

The second piece, written later, was a cathartic and therapeutic response to the onslaught of pain after the loss of a member of the order Carnivora, species Canis lupus familiaris, my dog Izzy. (For my part, the most telling component of this classification is the familiaris. From this word, we can extract the words familiar and family.) In this piece, I explored the connection between a specific member of Homo sapiens, myself, and a specific member of Canis lupus familiaris, Izzy, and attempted to draw some generalizations, not only about the relationship, but also about coming to terms with aging. There is a presumed directional dominance in the relationship between the two species, and at one level, Man clearly dominates over the dog with his power of reason and his ability to control his environment. But at another level, a more instinctual and emotional level, a degree of mutuality and equality exist, in which dog and human become interdependent, where each generates joy and sadness in the soul of the other. It is at this level, perhaps, that a story about the death of a father and a story about the death of a dog no longer seem like odd bedfellows—they both can and did occur in the heart of a member of Homo sapiens. A human heart bonds to living entities that bond to it. When these bonds are severed or substantially changed, a human cannot help but experience a sense of loss in a human way. These stories are connected because both were about living creatures that I allowed into my heart unconditionally, and during the same year, I had to let them go.

The story about my dog, Izzy, though it was written chronologically second, is the first piece in the book, and it is in length, at least, the far more substantial piece. I endured some shame in silence while my dog Izzy was dying, because the experience consumed such an extraordinary amount of my emotional energy and my time. I believed throughout that I had no business feeling as strongly as I did about a dog with all the human suffering in the world; yet my concern continued to overflow. I have since come to grips with this level of sentimentality, much of it as a result of writing "Of Human and Canine Bonds." It was the more difficult and painful journey of the two, with deeper peaks and valleys, creating moments of pure joy and profound pathos, lending an intensity to my human life that one sees in color before and after the sunset. It is a piece that could stand alone. I no longer feel shame that it is first, that it is longer, and that at some level, it tells of a more painful loss than my father earlier in the year. The piece about my father could stand alone, but it would not make up a book. Ultimately, these pieces do belong together because they are pieces of the same human heart from the same human era. Only one was extracted from my heart with a greater ripping sound.

The metaphor of "Diving Into Sunsets" is intended to draw your attention to the unique intensity, beauty, and pathos that accompanies the end of the day of a loved one's life. Attending to the dying and departed is one of the essential parts of living. We wish that we would never have to face it; we avert our eyes from it like we would from blinding direct sunlight. Yet we are always aware at some level of our "here and now" that mortality is there; we must carry on in the face of it, and in many ways, live our lives much closer to their limits because of it.

When we surrender ourselves to the care of a dying loved one, we offer a wonderful and sometimes draining gift, but not without reward, some expected and some unexpected. There can be terrible, incandescent moments of beauty just before the light of day is extinguished; and when the light of day is gone and the suffering have found their peace, the afterglow of a loved one can surround and inhabit us. So we need not blind ourselves looking directly into the sunlight; we can look upon what the sun, just about to slip below the horizon, illuminates— the batting of clouds, the naked trees, and the vast heavens above and opposite. And once life has passed below the horizon, the spirit of the human or canine loved one remains; it remains in our hearts and mind without the need to avert our eyes from the blinding sun. I know that this terminal beauty may not penetrate the pall of clouds that sits on the horizon for many, and that night follows the dying embers of the sunset for others. I can only hope that after this interminable night that another dawn arrives.

I want to make another comment about the metaphor in the title. I contemplated using the word "Leaping" into Sunsets instead of "Diving" into Sunsets. Both share an element of courage and composure. Diving requires a head first entry, and leaping permits a feet-first entry and perhaps requires less courage in the minds of many. We "dive" into our work, as the expression goes, and much of the care of our dying loved ones is work, if nothing else, often without thinking about the consequences to ourselves—and I wanted to emphasize this. But "leaping" implies an element that "diving" may not, the element of the "unknown". We must take a genuine "'leap' of faith" when we accept the responsibility of making the life of a loved one as meaningful as humanly possible. There is so much we do not know. We do not know of what and how much our loved ones will suffer. We do not know of what and how much we will suffer. We do not know when and if there will be respite moments of joy and grace. We do not know when it will end (though we have some control of this with a dog). And we certainly do not know what the end will look like. All this said, my hope remains that "diving" embodies enough of this element of the unknown as does "leaping", because taking care of dying loved ones is a great deal of work in the face of the unknown.

    The grim reaper wields his implement in many ways. For most, in this day and age, he affords a natural death, allowing a life to pass its natural day from sunrise to sunset, though some receive a shorter mid winter's day and others a summer solstice's day. "Natural death" may come in many forms, with names like kidney failure, cancer, or pneumonia. A death that occurs suddenly and unexpectedly, before the sun has the opportunity to decline in the sky and linger on the horizon, we consider less natural. It is newsworthy often, like the assassination of Lincoln, the tragic death of a child or young mother in an auto accident, or a youth fallen in battle for his country's cause; the list is endless and heartrending. These lives end as the light of day disappears in an eclipse, a tornadic cloud, or an asteroid collision. There is no time to expect, wait, and watch and live through it like a sunset. There may be some similarities in the ends of all lives, but this book has more to do with the joy and grief around lives of loved ones that end in sunsets.

Few people are mentioned by name in this book. My own name occurs infrequently. The first piece is addressed to my dog, Izzy, so his name occurs all the time. My wife's name, Cindy, also occurs because she is a protagonist in the story of my life. But I manage to complete both works without mentioning any other names, just identifying their relationship to me e.g. my older sister, or the service they provide e.g. veterinarian or physician assistant. Yet, a couple people and an organization ought to be recognized. My hometown veterinarian was outstanding. She was remarkably accessible and generous with her time; she was a fine diagnostician and an ideal guide through a difficult time for a pet owner. May you all find similar assistance with the non-human members of your family. The organization that I would like to recognize is frequently mentioned with deep admiration and gratitude by those who accept its services for a dying human loved one. This organization is hospice, comprised of a group of individuals dedicated to a single objective, making the passage of a human being at the end more comfortable and humane, both physically and spiritually—this applies not only to the patient, but to the family as well. Throughout my father's final day, a hospice nurse was available to me by phone, and this was only the tail end of the service that they provided to my father and family. She raised the right questions at the right time, and she was a voice of calm experience when my own generated doubt.

But I would like to extend my deepest gratitude related to all phases of this endeavor to my wife, Cindy. She not only contributed the photos to this book and assured its publication, but she also was part and parcel of the human mind and heart that created the beautiful micro-universe that surrounded the dying and death of our dog. Without her creativity and steadfastness, and her ability to recognize what is humanly moving, these experiences would have remained a word document.

OF HUMAN CANINE BONDS OR MY LIVING BOND WITH A DYING DOG

Izzy, we planted you beneath an eight-foot dogwood today at the front edge of our son's overgrown garden. The dogwood will live on as a memorial to the gift your life was to Cindy and me. Though its near winter nakedness blends into the background of mature tree trunks and overcast sky, we will someday soon see it clearly from the kitchen window when it flowers and leafs out. Giving you back to the earth was inexplicably the most painful thing I have experienced since my high school girlfriend broke up with me in my junior year. Anticipating the moment of your death after we decided to "put you down" made me ill with grief, for which your very infirm, but breathing presence was the only salve. The contents of a 12 cc syringe extinguished the last bit of life that was glued to our every move until the end. We gave you back to the earth today and the dogwood will hold your spirit for now.

The image of your lifeless body flattened beneath a two-foot layer of tamped sand and the heavy ball of dogwood roots and soil haunts me. If nothing else, in life, you were an extremely handsome, robust dog. You cannot possibly remain so beneath all this weight. The sheet that protected our sofa from your sandpapery paws in which you are wrapped cannot protect you from this onslaught. Though the sand at the depth of your final resting place seemed relatively free of living matter, it probably will not be long before insect larvae and saprophytes leave behind your beautiful pelt and crushed bones like road kill (I am having a hard time imagining that the curve of your rib cage will remain intact beneath the dogwood which took three grown men to lift a foot). Such maudlin and macabre images. Izzy, my Methuselah dog, I will miss you and cherish you more than even I can understand.

****

You were not a well-behaved dog. I do not know how many times I apologized for your behavior and how many more times I should have. You made it difficult, if not impossible for the friends of your human brothers, our two sons, to socialize in the living room or kitchen, because you harassed their friends nipping their hands or humping their legs; you were generally, an obnoxious, barking dog. You chased all their friends into the basement or to their bedrooms. I could not excuse this behavior, but I, more than anyone, accepted you for the naughty dog you were and maintained the same loyalty to you that you had for me.

You also were not a very neighborly dog. You allegedly, in your younger roaming days, snuck up on our neighbor and startled her with a vicious bark every night through the sliding door window of her basement. You barked and snarled as you snapped at the moving tires of our neighbor's cars that took off down their driveway; once you were knocked fifteen feet when the car suddenly accelerated to outwit you. If you were outside, you charged anyone who arrived at our neighbor's house and assaulted him with your territorial bark. You ignored us for years when we tried to retrieve you from your obnoxious behavior. Fortunately, you never bit anyone, because that would have been the end of you.

But you were a handsome dog, and that allowed us to overlook enough of your ugly behavior. You had an ideal combination of the features of a Golden Retriever and a Yellow Labrador Retriever--the red ears and red highlights of the Golden Retriever blended into the full blond coat of the Yellow Lab, thick and long like the Golden; the narrow, longer snout of the Golden on the broader head of the Lab; the longer legs of a Golden supporting the full shoulders of the Lab; and the size of both of them combined. You had the intense eyes of a hunter when focusing on a rock, and the eyes of a puppy dog when appealing for our meals. Many times, when we walked with you, onlookers admired your canine beauty. Humans may be suckers for blonds, but in your case, you really were the complete physical package.

Your mature behavior has nearly eclipsed your obnoxious younger behavior. You barked, you humped, you chased, you begged, and you listened consistently only when there was some fury in the command. You flunked obedience school with our help. We were told that you would mellow by two or three, but you were well into your second decade before your naughty motor began to rev down. When you were young, though on a pinch collar, you pulled hard enough that most people thought that you were taking us for a walk. But by your second decade, you were less insistent, and compared to your former self, you sauntered and took the time to smell dog roses, the scent of other dogs. As our walks with you wound down, we had to pull you sometimes, and we sacrificed our aerobic pace so that you could maintain your aging body.

Retrieving boulders at our family retreat in Suttons Bay, a hamlet fifteen miles north of Traverse City, Michigan, revealed both your obsession and your joy. Two months before you lay nearly motionless, you were still bobbing for rocks in the shallow water near the shoreline of Suttons Bay, and a month before, in the surf of Lake Michigan in South Haven at the mouth of Deer Lick Creek. At Suttons Bay, we could throw any stone large enough to make a noticeable splash and you would bring back a boulder that filled your large, gaping mouth. One time you frightened me when you could not release the stone, but somehow I managed to withdraw it gently. You returned with boulders that must have weighed up to 15 pounds, usually covered on the upside with algae slime. In your earlier days, you carried each of the boulders up the 12 or so steps from the beach to the back yard, and paraded around the yard so that everyone in sight noticed your feat. You finally would release the rock, and go down for another one (because there was an inexhaustible source of them), or if you were getting tired, you would settle with one of the larger rocks and chew on it, making an awful grating sound. Your teeth became stubs after a lifetime of this obsession, but it never slowed your appetite or ability to inhale all your favorite foods.

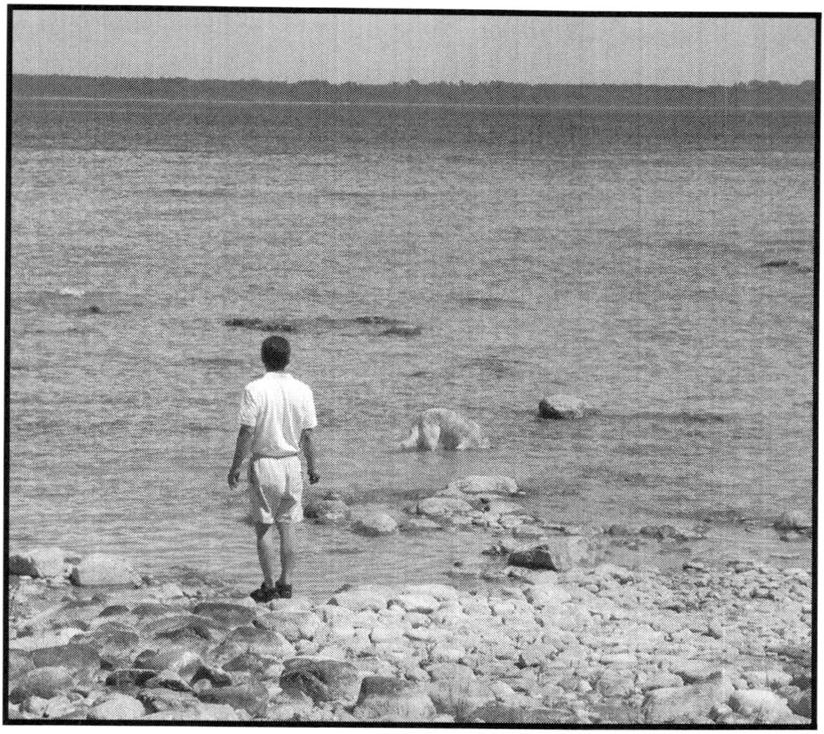

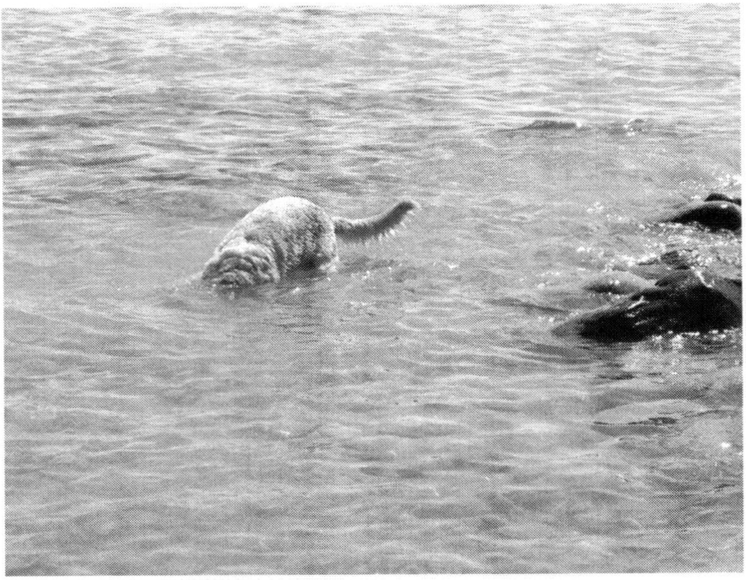

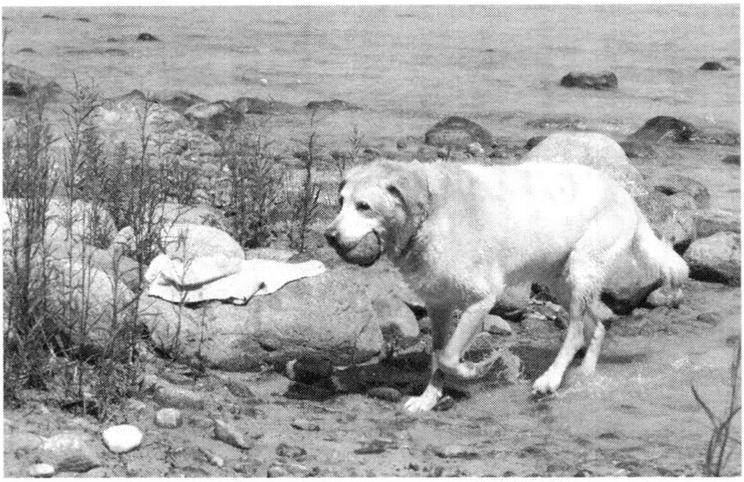

One time, in your younger days, I counted over two hundred

boulders scattered around the back yard. When we tired of throwing rocks before you tired of fetching them, you usually kept on diving for rocks. At first, we imagined no purpose for all the boulders you strew over the yard, perceiving them only as a nuisance. But as the habit grew on us and we saw you slowing down, I conceived of an Izzy Memorial. When our sons were toddlers, Cindy and I became concerned that they would tumble off a 6-foot high concrete retaining wall that bordered the back yard and protected it from the onslaught of November storms during the high water era of Lake Michigan. Huge boulders for which the pliable bones of our sons were no match rested at the bottom of this wall. To protect them, my brother, dad, and I built a two-foot tall, three-foot wide planter made of womanized timbers along the top of this wall. We intended to fill it with stones and dirt and plant a low growing groundcover like ivy, but never got around to it. Even empty, it served its purpose as a barrier to innocent eyes.

This planter, empty for a decade, became the repository for the Izzy Memorial. I encouraged everyone to collect the boulders that you retrieved from Grand Traverse Bay and to place them in the planter. By the time I conceived of your memorial, your pace of retrieval had slackened considerably (no more 200 boulder weekends) and your efforts filled this 70-foot long planter very slowly. Also, as the years passed, rather than encroaching upon our back yard, the Grand Traverse Bay inexplicably retreated, leaving an expanding field of boulders and fibrous weeds between the wall and the water's edge. You decided to conserve your energy and carried only the most satisfying rocks to the upper level of the back yard. The rest, you carried to this expanding field of weeds and previously submerged boulders, and either left them there or curled up with them and gnawed on them. Usually, I kept watch for these rocks, before they dried off and blended in with all the other boulders that a previous Ice Age had deposited in Northern Michigan. Toward the end, when you were more likely to curl up in the weeds with the rock, I had to coax it from you, walk it to the wall, and heave it like an undersized lead basketball into the opening of the planter. At times, you were possessive of your find and snapped it back up before I could get it (if you were able without the buoyancy of the lake) and wandered the beach with it. If you left it as I ordered, you would get up, shimmy yourself dry, and follow me and your prize to the wall, just to make sure I did not throw it into the lake to restart your cycle of retrieving. I could not watch you all the time, and I am sure that I missed a dozen or so rocks that became part of our weed and stone shoreline.

Retrieving boulders rejuvenated you like no other activity. You could be limping from a sore elbow or a painful hip, but as soon as you noticed someone walking down the steps of the back deck across the 30 feet of back yard, you instantly lost 5 years of wear and tear. The limp disappeared, and instead of sauntering, your natural and preferred pace, you ran again. It was almost worth interrupting anything I was doing to respond to your insistent nagging and watch this life re-enter you. It was one of those little miracles of life that injects moments of contagious joy. To the end, once you started retrieving, even as old age crept into your bones, you had a hard time stopping until you were completely deserted on the stony beach. As long as you had company, you kept it up. Toward the end when deafness silenced your world and you aged faster than the humans around you, you did not need anyone to throw a stone. In fact, to save your deteriorating joints and limbs, Cindy gave me a strict order to stop throwing stones to eliminate the inevitable dash over the treacherous rocky shoreline toward the splash of the stone.

When you were young and the water in Suttons Bay was higher, I would take a handful of stones and launch them from the top of the wall. I would toss the larger stones first because

I knew that they would create a big enough splash to entice you into the water. However, as my stone stash shrunk and your initial exuberance slackened, you demurred on the smaller stones. You darted a few steps, scoffed at the splash, and in a moment, your stare from the bottom of the wall again bored through me. I would then toss a handful of small stones, and occasionally, that would satisfy you. If I ignored your presence at the bottom of the wall for any period of time, your bark boomed. However, if I held a stone up and stood in the launch position, you fixed intently on the stone with steely patience; it was a unique depth of animal focus that I remember seeing also in one of the greatest linebackers on the Chicago Bears, Mike Singletary, just before the ball snapped. I enjoyed immensely giving you this animal pleasure. I believe that is part of the reason I grieve you so.

Your dive into the water was the most amazing part of the whole process. You bounded or dashed over the boulder-laden bottom of the shallow water toward the splash of the stone (your poor paws, bloodied at times). You would stop and get your bearings. Then using your front paws, you would get the feel of the landscape of the lake floor at the point the rock entered. If a boulder with potential moved beneath your paws, you scoped it out by dipping your snout and eyes in the water. Then you disappeared into the water, at times, leaving only a small patch of fur in front of your tail above water. You would stay submerged long enough that, at times, I thought you might drown in an effort to free up your prize and maneuver it into your mouth. As a rule, the longer you were under, the larger the boulder with which you emerged. As you hauled the rock to shore, the larger the rock, the louder you snorted as air eked around the rock in your mouth. As the lake level fell, your disappearing acts became less frequent and dramatic, but when you were fresh, you still never hesitated to tackle the tough rocks.

In your feisty youth, you set your front paws on your favorite flat boulder at the base of the wall while awaiting my throw from a lounge chair secured to the top of the planter.

When the bay water receded with your best years, I no longer had the luxury of throwing the stones from the top of the wall. I had to move to the water's edge, and at times, to a large boulder out in the water, to throw a rock into water deep enough that you could use the buoyancy of the water to pull a boulder up. Your bounding became a trot, and the nuisance rocks along the shore and in the shallow water became major obstacles for your feet. Still, you retrieved long enough that it took two days to recover your Methuselah strength and your usual level of discomfort. The limp that left you while rock-hounding rapidly returned in spades during recovery, and by evening, you lay in oblivious sleep, deaf to the world and insensible to your need to relieve yourself. Though you had slept in our room every night since you were a puppy, these rock-retrieving days left you so weary that we had to coax you multiple times to our bedroom in Suttons Bay.

After the 4 hour drive home from your final 2-week stay in Suttons Bay, you were so lame that you did not want to move from the back of our Odyssey van. You still would not move, even after resting while I unloaded the van. When we finally tugged you to the van's side door, you refused to make what must have seemed a giant step downward. We fashioned an intermediate step using concrete blocks, but you still resisted our tugs. I was alarmed by this new level of frailty; we had had problems getting you in the car, but never out of it. Finally, after over an hour, I saw no option but to pull you hard enough that you had to hobble out of the van. The episode suddenly ended without incident. Or the end was just beginning.

For days after we returned from Suttons Bay, you were unusually apathetic. We assumed that you sorely missed the bay's rocky abundance and that you had a bad case of the same transitional blues that afflicted both of us. Only later in the week did you emerge from your seeming depression when all of us rediscovered the treasures of South Haven, the beautiful beach stones at the mouth of Deer Lick Creek. Though your limp never again left you, we loaded you in the Odyssey and drove you to Deer Lick. You learned that South Haven's boulders are as plentiful as Suttons Bay's, and we learned that the stones of Deer Lick contrasted with those of Suttons Bay like color photography with black and white. Alternatively, in South Haven, we were over the Rainbow, and in Suttons Bay we were back in Kansas. In the pursuit of meeting your needs, we unlocked the gate to a minute patch of heaven.

We rediscovered the beach at Deer Lick with the beauty of its sunsets and the mysteriousness of dusk. Summer was over and the beach was usually deserted. Temporarily, it became our special island in time and space. You rock hounded in your usual way and we in ours. Cindy refined her eye for Petoskey stones and discovered that they were almost as plentiful on the southern end of Lake Michigan as the northern. For my part, my obsession for fossil stones up north morphed to one for arrangements of reds, yellows, oranges, greens, pinks and blacks, and for the sundry striped stones that were given their patterns by the laws of physics and chemistry rather than by an ancient coral or crustacean.

Unlike Suttons Bay, our obsession outlasted yours. We strained our eyes long after sunset to find the most beautiful or strange stone on the beach or in the water, filling our pockets and buckets with fingernail-sized pebbles to muskmelon boulders. Mainly the whites stood out in the afterglow of the sunset. You still seemed to enjoy yourself wandering between Cindy and me; I tended to remain with the dense concentration of stones and boulders near the mouth of the creek whereas Cindy hoped to find the holy grail stone washed up a quarter mile south. You were the glue between us, never out of our minds, the pursuit of your joy ultimately our reason to pursue ours. A late summer day would magically splinter on the horizon, followed by the deep blue shades of night. In the dying light, I would discover that while our eyes were focused on our treasure hunt, you had littered the beach with an array of boulders that stood out darkly on the white South Haven sand.

Before getting you in the van that was parked at the top of a sandy hill, I surveyed the long stretch of beach, the dark silhouettes of trees, and the green-black rippled sheen of water that merged with faded remnants of the sunset. Breezes, still mild and gentle, stroked us. I stood silent and apart, and meditated on the scene around me, waiting. Hopefully, a few more seconds would be enough; I did not want the evening to end, but I knew that it had to. I could leave if I could just experience that climactic moment, a distillation of what had already been a remarkable evening, when what I saw before me became our paradise alone, a paradise that could have been anywhere in the world—this beautiful place, miles away in time and space, somewhere between serenity and bliss. When it came, all my tethered worries broke loose and I felt free to live and free to die. Cindy too felt it and you, my Methuselah dog, were the core of our three being universe. You were wet and tired, but I can only imagine completely content.

We turned our attention to getting you in the van. Long before, you had lost the spring in your legs required to hop in through the back unless we backed up to a hill. But now, you hesitated to make the shorter step to the running board of the side doors. I opened both side doors to give you a choice. You walked up to one side and pushed your chest into edge of the floor; it took most of your energy, it seemed, just to contemplate making the step. When you walked away, we cajoled you back. You then lifted one of your front paws to the floor, but then could not imagine how to get the other three up. At the time, we did not know how to lift your hundred pound frame into the car in a way that would not cause you to yelp and resist. But we knew that if we both got in the car, turned on the engine and appeared ready to go, and then enticed you from our front seats, you would find the wherewithal to hop into the car. You were not yet ready to collapse from exhaustion, because, like the day, you were still in your afterglow—from rock hounding.

****

Not without difficulty, I accepted your losses from aging. What I accepted as a natural process in humans as a physician became a more difficult pill to swallow when it came to you. For years, I welcomed you into our bed at night. Cindy protested at first because you were an active sleeper, and when you finally settled down, you often sprawled out to occupy over half the bed. But even she grew accustomed to your presence, as you lost some of your youthful spunk and found your way to my side of the bed almost exclusively. I would not hesitate to accommodate you, curling into a ball or straightening into a board at the edge of the bed. I conceded an hour or more of sleep some nights to keep you comfortable.

One night, the summer before your last one up at Suttons Bay, you contemplated making the leap from the foot of our bed. A three-inch layer of egg crate foam raised this bed further from the ground than one to which you were accustomed in South Haven, and instead of launching from the sure footing of Berber carpet, you were forced to push off from slippery oak flooring. You managed to get your front paws on top of the blanket, but your back legs did not follow.

When you repositioned yourself for another unsuccessful attempt to get in bed, I came up from behind and tried to help lift your back legs. You fought my efforts and yelped in pain, and I gave up. The next day, you were limping, I believed, from the pounding of the boulders on your aging feet. Only later when I tried to lift you in the same way and you could hardly walk the following day did I realize that transferring all that weight to your front legs stretched your elbow beyond its capacity. The incident frightened you enough that you took to sleeping in your own bed at night and we lost your familiar overnight presence. I might have slept more soundly, but if it were possible, I would have turned back your clock, even if it meant accelerating my own from loss of sleep.

It took weeks before I gave in to Cindy's recommendation that we shorten your 3-mile walk by a mile or so. We continued our walk to Evergreen Bluff for a view of the Lake Michigan shoreline, but eliminated a less scenic stretch to and from Delaware Court. To put some pep in your step and cool you down, especially on hot days, we broke the walk up with a trip down to the beach at the end of Evergreen Bluff so that you might dive for boulders and cool off in the lake. (It was this decision that re-introduced the South Haven shoreline to Cindy and planted the seed for her rock hounding.) Walking you down to the beach over a pallet-covered path was probably the last time you tugged on your leash. When elbow pain caused you to limp after these walks, I finally agreed to Cindy's recommendation that we give you a day or two of rest between walks. I believed that these walks were essential to your weight-maintenance, health, and longevity, so that giving them up was for me, the beginning of giving you up.

The loss was bigger for me, however, than it was for you. For most of your life, you were unable to sit when anticipating your next morsel of food, your next walk, or your next trip in the car. Your uncontained excitement made you a nuisance with barking, jumping, and nipping, but as your exuberance waned, you began to walk your front legs down into a seated position while waiting for the next segment of your day. The disappearance of one of your defining obnoxious behaviors, I perceived as one of the perks of a maturing dog, but I mourned this change too.

You aged so gradually that others unacquainted with you had to point it out to me that you were covered with white hair. A small child who saw your picture on the wall at the office even remarked, "That dog must be really old." I asked, "What made you say that?" He had noticed the white mask of hair on your face. I thought that white mask had always been there. What is it that I had no trouble noticing the physical features of aging humans, but had overlooked changes in you that were obvious to others, the increasing sag of your physique and the whitening of your hair, expected in a dog closing in on 80 in converted human years? Unlike human flesh that is a barometer for age, the coat of a dog hides a million little flaws. Even as your breath took on the odor of rotten fish, you remained a beautiful animal in my eyes.

I accepted that you were officially a mature dog that could not do what he had done as a middle-aged dog. I knew that you were approaching your thirteenth birthday, the expected lifespan of a large retriever. But having heard stories from patients about their retrievers that lived to be 15 or 17 years old, I did not readily conclude that a switch would turn off at thirteen. Instead, I prepared myself for a gradual decline. Had I just watched you in your near deafness detect the honk of a flock of geese and chase them in Suttons Bay until you became a blond speck, frightening me that you might become weary and drown? But you returned refreshed. You still ravished your food, and aside from a few benign lumps beneath your fur, you seemed healthy for your age. So when your bladder failed, I figured if we took care of that problem, you would be good for a while yet.

****

We had not been back from Suttons Bay for longer than two weeks and were well entrenched in our South Haven existence, when Cindy first discovered a small puddle of fluid on the floor in the kitchen and suspected that it was your urine. I maintained that it was more likely your drool since just the thought of food had caused a flood of saliva many times in the past. Besides, in Suttons Bay, we had seen you hold your urine for almost 12 hours. After a day of fetching rocks, you collapsed on the rug shortly after sunset, and would not pee until the next morning. However, when we found more puddles with trails of dribble, I had to agree with Cindy. When we saw you squat and strain in the kitchen and leave a small puddle, we hustled you outdoors to finish the job. We were worried about your lack of bladder control, but we chalked it up to one of those occasional lapses that occurs in very old dogs. We soon noticed, however, that you were not only leaking in the house, but you were also squatting and straining to urinate, almost as if you were trying to have a bowel movement. What's more, you were just urinating piddling amounts.

This was just the beginning of an on-call Saturday that would extend long and excruciatingly into the gray dawn of Sunday. As a human physician, I naturally considered your symptoms from a human medical perspective. After all, you were a mammal that many times acted human; you had a bladder and a prostate that had grown old with the rest of you. If a human male presented with the same symptoms, I would have readily assumed that he had a urinary tract infection caused by an enlarging prostate that made it difficult to empty his bladder. I sought confirmation in my pet book library and on the Internet. I also went to the office to get a sterile urine cup to collect a urine specimen and then followed you around the yard collecting the dribble that escaped from your prepuce, the covering of your penis. After three tries, I collected barely enough to cover the bottom of the small plastic container. But it was enough to test at the office, both by dipping a test strip in it and by examining a centrifuged sample of it under the microscope. I found dilute urine clear of inflammatory cells and bacteria. I spilled the remaining urine on a culture strip and remained resolute, in spite of your clear urine, about my presumptive diagnosis that you were simply suffering from a bladder irritated by an infection.

On the Internet, I tried to determine if the antibiotics used in humans were appropriate in dogs at the same doses. Even before conferring with the veterinarian, I had Cindy pick up a couple of antibiotics that were used to treat dogs. But before giving you your first dose, I called the vet, more to confirm the proper antibiotic and dose, than to confirm my diagnosis of urinary tract infection. She believed that one of the antibiotics we selected was better than the other and confirmed a dose, and while believing that a urinary tract infection was the probable cause of your frequent urination in piddling amounts, she informed me that neutered dogs, especially Labs, rarely suffered from enlarged prostates, presumably because they do not have the male hormone to make the prostate grow. Nevertheless, at that moment, I felt reassured in my diagnosis and treatment plan, and gave you your first dose of antibiotics. While I did not expect the medication to cure you instantly, I did expect that it would halt the progression of your symptoms.

However, your behavior failed to reassure me. We had

become accustomed to your late-mature-years preference to spend all your quiet time lying down or sleeping, minimizing the number of times you had to walk your front legs straight and heave your back end to a standing position. Your present ailment, however, caused you to pace aimlessly and endlessly around the yard. You would try to rest comfortably for a few minutes in the house, but before long you made your way with little fanfare, no bark or whining, to the front door or to the sliding door leading to the back deck. As you left a puddle if we did not immediately let you out, we remained acutely alert to any time you got up and walked in the direction of a door. We had old large bath towels positioned in every area of our house to clean up the inevitable accidents. We eventually left the door to the screened-in porch open and the screen door exiting the porch ajar so that you could find your way to the side yard without our help. Even with this liberty to move in and out of the house, you rarely escaped our concerned watch.

By the end of the afternoon, you had leaked urine on all the carpets and most areas of the oak floor, sparing only the carpet in our dressing closet and most of my study. You began to leak when you lay down to rest your weary bones before the urge to urinate overwhelmed you again; it was not possible to get up without dribbling. By the time the afternoon raced away in frustration toward what would become an interminable night, I had begun to research new concerns. Was it possible that you were leaking all the time because you had overflow incontinence? Had your bladder become so full of urine that it no longer emptied at your command, but only when the excessive pressure of a certain volume forced some of your urine out? I searched the Internet without much success for information that would clarify my suspicions. I Googled all different combinations of the words, dog, urinary obstruction, etc. without finding definitive information that suggested a course of action. Cindy would later find an on-line forum that was helpful, but that came much later. As nightfall befell us, your problem had become the center of our universe. Cindy had decided most practically that we should spend the night on the porch with you to preserve our carpets and oak floors so that you would not have to suffer alone.

At the outset, we tried to insert a camping atmosphere into the uncertainty and misery. The night was mild and humid, the type that could put a wave in the paper of the finest hardback. We ate supper looking out on the lingering light of the late August sunset that pierced the overcast skies and the heavy foliage of the western side of our yard. Your discomfort was evident because you did not lie impatiently whining or barking as you usually did, awaiting the residue of baked bean glaze from my plate. Restive from your ailment, you found comfort in wandering in the yard. I left the plate on the lumber floor of the porch hoping that you would eventually do a better job cleaning my plate than you did your hardly-touched bowl of dog food in the kitchen.

We covered the floor of the porch with sleeping surfaces, an old single mattress and a thick foam pad, in the hope that you would find peace sleeping with us and snore through your pain. It had been a year since you had lost the spring to leap onto our bed and crowd our sleep. We brought out reading lights to make our eyelids heavy later on, if necessary. We tried to hook up the kitchen TV near the porch doorway to watch the Saturday night fare, but we gave up when the cable cord would not quite reach. Without a campfire, shortly after the last residue of daylight vanished, it seemed late. Cindy gave up on reading and, anticipating an interrupted night of sleep, decided to turn in. My night owl habits also took a back seat to your problem. It was a Saturday night before the eleven o'clock news aired, in the starless universe of your unknown ailment, and we were preparing for the unpleasant ordeal of interrupted sleep.

The night brought torment to all of us, though you, more than any of us, seemed to take your malady in stride. And stride you did for most of the night. Early on, you may have slept with us for half an hour or an hour, but during the remainder of the night, as soon as you tried to lower your haunch to the deck, you raised yourself back on your feet like you had sat on a bed of nails. While it seemed that lying on your side should have been a more comfortable alternative, this position brought you to your feet faster than lying prone. Innumerable times I watched helplessly as you disappeared down the steps of the porch into the black of the night. My anguish grew with each of these trips because I had become accustomed to your old-dog avoidance of lifting and supporting the heft of your body and your sleep marathons from evening into the next late morning.

Your stoicism flooded me with both pathos and admiration as I watched you push your haunches up without a moan and walk down the porch steps one more time. You should have collapsed in exhaustion, but you lumbered into the night again and again; you lumbered into the dark and you lumbered back from the dark. I had to follow your sojourns mainly by ear as the night collapsed around you thirty feet from the porch. Sometimes, you came back wet up to your knees after visiting the pond a few hundred feet down our gravel road to the north. I imagined that the late August pond water on your hindquarter was like a water bottle on a headache, or that the water, which you always loved, took you back to more carefree times. As the night wore on, you would disappear for variable amounts of time, lasting as long as a protracted fifteen minutes, but always coming back.

Still, I never completely convinced myself that you would always return; I tried to lie down and rest after letting you out but kept an ear attuned to your staccato panting and the faint jingle of your choke collar. When I heard you, I bounced up to open the screen door that was left ajar to let you out, but had to be opened to let you in. Many times, I heard your wandering close by without seeing you and would call you in vain. Long ago you had become deaf to the sounds that influenced much of your behavior in a Pavlovian way, like the opening of the refrigerator door or the words, "guard the house", which meant that you were going to get a treat before I left the house. Each time, I was thrilled to see my majestic, large blond beast reappear in stages from the darkness of the night. In your stoic agony you cut the same heroic figure as the ancient African elephant in Tarzan movies that lumbered off alone to face his Maker among the worn tusks and spirits of the magnificent beasts that preceded him.

    In spite of our efforts to make the porch your home for the night, it became more like a prison cell for you. We had to block your attempts to go into the house for obvious reasons and you found more comfort wandering the yard than lying beside us in bed. At the outset, we envisioned that you would sleep on your dog bed which we moved from our bedroom, and that we would sleep on the unfamiliar cushions we brought up from the basement. Cindy gave me the more comfortable old mattress while she took a thick foam pad, but she did not last as long into the night and returned to our bedroom. The porch was a jigsaw puzzle with these makeshift beds with barely a footpath between. At first, we enforced a one bed, one animal policy, blocking any of your attempts to get into our beds. I was the first to give in to your natural tendency to climb into our beds. Opening our beds to you was no small concession. You were wet and sandy from your excursions to the pond; you were leaking urine; and you were constantly on the move with discomfort. Still, when I saw that our mere company was giving you no relief and you wanted our beds too, I tried to assume any position, even curled up in an area the size of my pillow to give you enough room to stretch into some comfort. This was one of my many unsuccessful attempts to absorb some of your pain in the hope of putting life back into you. Instead of giving you sleep, our beds became damp and gritty and tattooed with paw prints. Even Cindy's unoccupied foam pad did not give you relief. As morning drew near, it was painfully obvious that there was nothing that we could do to give you relief.

When the first hint of dawn appeared in the Eastern sky, it provided the relief of a narcotic finally kicking in after hours of suffering from a toothache. Still, the night could have been worse. The beeper that I wore to cover my medical practice had remained silent all night. The heavy air that dampened all night sounds except the strange birdcall of a nocturnal mammal and the trucks from Blue Star a half mile away, produced no more than a brief mist and a stillness that made it easy to follow your movements in the dark. Most importantly, you had shown an unexpected resilience in your ability to pace most of the night and still had life left in the morning. Light in the eastern sky, most importantly, meant that others who might provide assistance would soon awaken. We could finally admit others into our exclusive and tortured universe.

I waited until what I thought was a decent hour to phone the veterinarian on call. By that time, your behavior had convinced me that you had more than a bladder infection, and in all probability, had an obstruction that would not allow your bladder to drain. It would be days before I found out the true consequence of this obstruction, though we would never find out its cause with certainty. An associate of our local veterinarian was kind enough, but she introduced possible explanations for your malady that I had not considered which included catastrophic bowel problems that both alarmed me and did not make sense to me; additionally, she was not available to see you for hours because of other commitments. Only after talking to an intake nurse at an animal hospital in nearby city did I feel that I had talked to someone who understood your problem. After hearing all the details of the last 24 hours, particularly that your symptoms seemed to have come on suddenly—absent the evening before and present the next morning—she thought that it was highly likely that you had a blockage in your urethra, the tube that drains your bladder, and that the probable cause of this blockage was a stone. Her manner of assurance gave me more relief than the sunrise. I thought that there was a place I could take you and not only give you relief, but also fix you.

Had I known how profoundly relaxed you would become in the car during the 40 mile drive to the animal emergency room, I would have driven you around in the Honda Odyssey all night. Your panting ceased and you collapsed on your side. You even hopped into the car with your usual zest, as most times lately, a trip in the car meant that we were heading to a beach with rocks. Better than rocks, we hoped you would find some relief.

****

The animal hospital was a small, plain building on a side street of one of the main thoroughfares in a city large enough to have a large state university and a highly regard private college. When you walked into the bare waiting room, you were the only emergency to which they had to attend and you received the personal attention and the sincere admiration that I thought you deserved. I recounted all the details of the last 24 hours to the veterinarian on call. She reminded me of a strikingly tall long-time patient of mine, only more attractive with smoother skin and a less prominent nose. Unlike my patient who had no erudite airs, the veterinarian, while inspiring confidence, at times strained my sleep-deprived mind with medical jargon. From the information that I gave her, she concluded that you probably had a stone lodged in the bone of your penis. Eventually, she would show me on an x-ray of your hindquarters what she meant by "a bone in your penis". After she had instructed me about the anatomy of the canine penis, I remarked straight-faced that the males of the population with which I worked had "boners", but no bones in their penises. The off-colored comment went by unnoticed until Cindy expressed her disbelief with a slight guffaw in the car on the way home.

The vet informed us that passing a catheter through your penis could relieve your discomfort and give her information about the degree of your obstruction. If possible, she was going to try the procedure without sedation. That sounded good to me--less invasion, less risk, less money. She and her associate led you away to a no-frills surgical suite with a central metal table, out of sight and out of earshot. Had I been a smoker, I would have had time to smoke a few before the vet found us in the waiting room and took us into a small supply room that connected the lobby with the emergency suite. She reported with some satisfaction that she was able to pass the catheter without any anesthesia and had, in fact, done it twice. With the first catheter that had turned out to be too short, she had had to overcome some resistance. The second catheter slid through without any difficulty. At the time, I believed that passing a catheter into a large dog, aside from guts, took considerable skill and experience, and I was very thankful for the news. The vet also reviewed a special x-ray using contrast that showed the contour of your urethra and also your bladder. Your urethra looked clear of any stones but she did not have enough contrast material to fill and distend your bladder to view its contour. Unlike the aging human male, you did not appear to have an enlarged, obstructing prostate.

The vet's theory was that you had a stone in your urethra that she had dislodged and pushed back into the bladder with the first catheter insertion. There were other possibilities like a neurogenic bladder, a bladder that functions poorly because of damaged nerves, but the stone hypothesis seemed most likely based on my description of the events. Unfortunately, the bone in your penis created a problem in management that is not present in humans. Ordinarily, a stone in the bladder of a human male will either pass freely with a brief period of burning, or vegetate in the bladder and occasionally cause some bleeding. If the stone ever did require removal, a urologist could easily pass a scope into the bladder and, if necessary, crush the stone. However, a stone in a dog's bladder must be removed surgically by making a small incision into the abdominal wall and then through the bladder. Passing a scope through the rigid bony part of the dog's penis could injure the lining irreparably.

On the heels of this discussion came another one that would not occur in an aging human with one impaired organ. Rather than merely discussing the diagnostic and therapeutic procedures necessary to heal you, the vet showed us a sheet that listed the estimated cost of your anticipated hospitalization and procedures. It is possible that another pet owner may have looked at the finances and determined that you were not worth the cost. Pet owners, without the constraints of a complex legal framework that govern the options available to humans, must make life and death decisions regarding their pets; the absence of an insurance plan for aging dogs similar to Medicare also necessitated this discussion regarding finances. The sum of seven hundred dollars and change for items that included, among other things, a day or two in the hospital, an IV and IV fluids, anesthesia for your x-ray test, the material for your x-ray test, the x-ray test itself, and the catheters and catheterization, did not seem exorbitant, especially if we knew how to fix you at the end of it. The surgery, if necessary, would cost about $500 dollars more. It all seemed reasonable to us, even paying half of the highest estimate up front. Well-cared-for pets are luxuries that feel much more like necessities when it comes to losing them.

After these discussions ended painlessly, I asked if I could see you before we left. Cindy and I had not seen you since the vet and her assistant walked you away, and I wanted you to know that we were still in the building concerned about you. Whether, you as a dog needed to know that we still cared, I do not know. For me, it was natural when trying to empathize with you to personify you in the form of a child, because our attachment to a dog is more like the one to a child than to a parent or a partner; we take care of you like one of our pre-schoolers, and for our regular attendance, we receive undying loyalty.

When I mentioned my desire to see you before we left, Cindy thought it was a bad idea. She thought that it would excite you unnecessarily and make you want to come home with us when you had no option but to stay in the hospital. She said, "Think about Izzy and his needs. Not your own." I thought that I was thinking about your needs. You needed to know that we were not deserting you and that we still cared about you. Had I thought that leaving without seeing you would have been easier for you, I have no doubt that I would have left right away. At that moment, all I wanted was what was best for you. I had no doubt then that I would eventually see you again soon.

I do not regret going into that procedure room even though Cindy was right about your response. When I walked in the room before you saw me, you lay limply stretched out on your left side. You looked profoundly exhausted, awake, but still dead to the world. Knowing the unusual amount of energy you expended the evening and night before, I did not think anything would breathe life into you at that moment. It could have been that you had surrendered to the strange circumstances, the operating table onto which they somehow had lifted you, the room's sterile features, and the strange humans unsheathing your penis and shoving a tube up the opening that you used to assert your canine dominance. You could not have heard me enter, but when your lifeless eyes saw me, you sprung back to life and struggled to get up. I was glad that you cared enough to use the last bit of energy to respond to one of your masters, but I withdrew immediately; I cannot remember if I touched you. I can only hope that my brief visit raised your spirits a bit and that I was not being self-centered; I always did treat you more like a human than Cindy, so you must forgive me for humanizing your needs.

Your hospitalization did not accomplish what we had hoped it would. At a minimum, we thought that the staff would perform the appropriate diagnostic tests necessary to identify why you could not urinate. We also left that bleak Sunday morning with the expectation that they might fix your problem as well. We were to be disappointed on both accounts. With profuse apologies and some embarrassment on two consecutive days, the veterinarian who admitted you told us that she was unable to secure enough contrast, or dye, to do the x-ray study necessary to find out if you had stones in your bladder. Since the difficulty obtaining contrast extended your hospitalization, in fairness to us and to assuage my frustration, she promised to subtract a day of charges from your hospitalization. This contrast material was not rare like cobalt, or platinum. Human hospitals have gallons of the material and I did not understand why a referral animal hospital in a decent sized city could not come up with the quantity necessary to do your study. A couple days later, my local veterinarian would have no trouble finding enough contrast to do your study.

The hospital veterinarian did take the time to give me lengthy updates. As I accepted the role of patient by proxy, these conversations took place at her convenience and only after I had made several phone calls inquiring about your status, talking to staff members that were less informed and less interested in you than those at our initial encounter. I supposed that the animal hospital had the same uneven quality in their front office staff as exists in any medical office. From these conversations, I gathered that you were gradually doing better. She was able to report on your urine stream based upon her own observations. As nurses usually report on the elimination status of human patients, I thought this was quite thorough of her. I did not consider, however, that those who usually walk the animals and watch them eliminate might have the greatest expertise on such matters. She explained that dogs usually urinate in pulses. That made sense to me; that's how you carried on your pissing contests. Your urine stream had progressed from a brisk trickle of droplets to a weak stream and was beginning to show early signs of developing a pulse. It was not normal yet, but she left me with the impression that it was getting there.

After two days of accomplishing little other than creating a void in our own home, with the apology and partial approval of the vet, I decided to bring you home after work on a Tuesday. I was under the impression that your urine stream was good enough to keep your bladder empty. I was willing to take the risk that a stone might still be in your bladder and would again enter your urethra and lodge in the bony portion of it. But I knew that your time on earth and our time with you were more finite than ever, and that I was not willing to waste another day of it waiting for a test that might not happen. If a problem were to arise, it would occur during the week when I could take you to your own local vet.

Cindy and I went together to pick you up. They had

moved you across the street to a new facility that had a larger waiting area and felt less personal, more like a real emergency room. The staff at the time once again knew very little about you and your care. They were responsible for collecting payment for your care, but they were unable to explain the details of the bill and eventually had to disappear into the treatment area of the facility to get answers to my questions. I had found unexpected charges for sedation and the insertion of a second catheter. The veterinarian had been able to insert the catheter without sedation and she had been unable to obtain the x-ray study that required sedation. In the end, my inquiry only served to delay your return to our care; the staff took what seemed like forever to find a veterinarian who knew about your care, and, at the time, had animals and pet owners with more pressing needs than yours and mine. We ended up paying the entire bill that was very close to the quote that included the x-ray. We learned that sedation was required to place a second urinary catheter when you had pulled out your first one, because the veterinarian on call at that time did not want to replace it without sedating you. At the time, without mentioning it, I held the facility responsible for allowing you to pull the catheter out. Later on, we would learn only too well that you required no more than a muzzle to settle you down to place a catheter, but that it was impossible, on the other hand, to keep a catheter in you for any period of time.

You were too distracted by the strange place with strange animals and people to take part in the dramatic reunion with us that I had imagined. Your torso did not gyrate in the joy of seeing us nor did you have the knowing glint in your eye of Odysseus's dog after his master returned from his travels. The staff returned you to us with an unfamiliar collar, and once more, one of them disappeared into the treatment area long enough to push us closer to the edge. A hospitalization that had started so auspiciously with caring personnel, a known mission, and a probable outcome, was almost at an end. We just had to get you into the van, after allowing you to leave your singular scent on the young shrubs outside.

Only then did I learn how imperfect the hospitalization had been and that its only purpose had been to take you from our midst for two precious days. You lifted your leg in the usual manner and only after few seconds of exertion did a dribble begin followed by a brief squirt. It seemed that the stream, weak but steady, like an old man's, existed only in my imagination. Perhaps that squirt at the end amounted to a pulse, but your veterinarian had described a brisk trickle that had progressed to a weak stream. My distress was eased only by having you back in our midst and by the hope that I had not yet seen your bladder's best.

As I drove out of the parking lot, I had hope that life for you would return to some sort of normalcy. To promote this view of the future and to erase the stench of the past two days, I proposed to use the waning evening light at the Deerlick beach in South Haven. Cindy did not believe it would have quite the salutary effect that I did, but she consented. She believed that I had foolishly adopted her favorite Aunt Norma's superstition about the healing powers of water which her aunt confirmed years earlier when she had sprained her ankle severely enough that she could hardly walk on it. During a trip to the New Jersey beach, her aunt insisted, though her girth was becoming prohibitive, that the men in the group carry her to the ocean's surf so that she could take its healing saltwater. The story became part of the family lore and a defining moment for her aunt. To my dismay, the Deerlick beach did not have the intended healing effect that the saltwater did for Aunt Norma. The sparkle and intensity that water and rocks usually brought to your gaze did not return. You remained too preoccupied with emptying the half-gallon of water in your own system to pay attention to vast body of it all around you.

****

The next 36 hours would bring us back to the same depth of torment that had precipitated the visit to the animal emergency room. However, this time, our local veterinarian, who had heard about your saga from her local associate, came to our rescue. Our local veterinarian left a message on our answering machine, giving us permission to call her at home, if necessary. Respectful of her time off as she had always been of mine, I was initially hesitant to call her at home. When I did finally call because of mounting discomfort from your inability to empty your bladder, I was surprised to learn that she had already spoken to your treating veterinarian at the animal hospital. She had nothing but good things to say about your treating vet at the hospital. Frustrated with the whole of my experience at the hospital, but not specifically with hospital veterinarian, I did not try to refute your local veterinarian's account. But I did mention my surprise and gratitude for going above and beyond the call of duty to make this phone call and to invite me to call her at home. Your local veterinarian had not yet seen you for this problem and, unlike the ER, she had not been the beneficiary of one cent from your malady. And she led me to believe that she did this for many of her clients. If so, many in her community owe her more than their gratitude.

It's not that she ended up performing a miracle for you like a thoracic surgeon who gives new life to an oxygen-deprived heart muscle or a plastic surgeon who removes a disfiguring facial cancer without leaving a trace of his work. These specialists are merely performing their job, using their natural talents and training, to perform what the layperson might consider a miracle. The medical and lay communities recognize the depth and rarity of their skills and compensate them appropriately. But they are not going out of their way to perform these "miracles." On the other hand, my veterinarian, on her own time and dime, scrounged our community for the contrast material necessary to perform the x-ray test that for two days the city animal hospital had been unable to obtain. When your case turned out to be more or less unique, she consulted by phone with three other specialist veterinarians to obtain their opinions about how to manage your problems. Her actions added hours, perhaps days, to the time we had to enjoy your life on this planet, by saving us from traveling across the state to get another opinion, which we were prepared to do for you.

Your local veterinarian did not attempt to relieve my distress by offering false reassurances or by delivering wise and warm counseling. She did not fawn all over you like there was not another dog like you in the entire country. Once, when she entered the room, she addressed you by saying, "I know that I am not your favorite person." At one point in your perplexing case, she admitted that she found your case a great one for learning. I took no offense at this, but this comment embodies the attitude that disturbed me greatly during my internal medicine rotation in medical school because "a great case" focused the student on the medical ailment rather than the person with the ailment. But I wanted her to pursue cutting edge information and treatment for your problem. I wanted you to be something special in her mind.

Though we were able to make a tentative plan if your malady should reach another crisis, coordinating your care with the schedules of the humans in your life and obtaining all the necessary equipment was still complicated. Cindy worked all day as a teacher. I had patients scheduled and could not desert them. The day after you came home from the hospital, it became increasingly clear that little had changed as a result of your care there. You were urinating constantly and it only trickled out with a brief squirt at the end, a pattern that would become painfully familiar. You were not leaking as much all over the house, but we constantly had to be aware of where you were to know if you needed to go outside. Overnight, I had remained in a semi-wakeful state so that I could jump out of bed if I heard stirring from your bed or your nails shuffling down the wooden floor of the hallway. I raced to the front door so that you would not piddle in the entryway. By morning, once again, you could not withstand putting your weight on your hindquarters.

I reached a state of desperation once again, tempered only by knowing that your local veterinarian was available and that I had only a half-day of patients at the office. But still, Cindy had a whole day of classes to teach and I still had to wade through a morning of patients when I felt there was nothing more urgent than finding you relief. Cindy and I tried to make a plan for you while each of us raced through our morning routines to get ready for the day. But watching you try to get comfortable on your hindquarters before you decided to go outside again distracted me. My own appetite faded when you ate as if any food in your stomach would put pressure on your bladder. Even your usual insatiable thirst was tempered by the instinctual connection you were making between the water you guzzled and the expanding water balloon in your hindquarters. Had my own morning routine not been instinctual, my anguish over your condition would have foiled me. My shower passed with me wondering whether I shampooed my hair, I was so lost in my thoughts trying to fit your needs into a busy day.

Cindy thought that it would be best if we left you outside so that you could relieve yourself whenever you desired. She was thinking more about your comfort than the carpets, even though cleaning the carpets had fallen upon her after your first bout. I never did express outright approval of her idea, and only mentioned my concerns that you might wander off or feel punished that we left you outside when you were more comfortable inside. All along, I was formulating a plan, to myself, since we had already decided that I would take you to the veterinarian. It was my half-day, and as part-owner of my medical practice, I could modify my schedule. Since you had done so well in the van on the way to the animal hospital a few days earlier, I was considering a plan in which I put you in the back of the van and let you rest there until I could take you to the veterinarian. I could check on you regularly between patients and walk you among the weeds at the edge of the parking lot. If I became too busy, I could ask one of the nurses to walk you; many of them learned about your condition when they had seen how distraught I was while you were in the hospital. I was still mulling this idea by the time Cindy left for school, but had not yet mentioned it to her. I simply did not know if I could pull it all together.

When I was finally ready to leave for work after lugging my stacks of medical charts to the car and letting you out to pee one more time, it was almost as if I had conceived of the idea of keeping you in the van at that moment; in a flash, I knew that you and I could pull it off. I drove the van down to the bottom of the short incline in front of our house so that the back of the van would be closer to the ground. I got your leash and led you down to the tailgate. I relied on your belief that every car ride was potentially a trip to the beach as motivation to lift your waterlogged body into the back of the van. It was the happiest you had been in the last 20 hours. The urine soaked cardboard and blanket from our ride to the animal hospital were still drying in the back of the van. Once again, the anticipation of what a car ride brings alleviated enough pain that you could rest comfortably for the first time in hours. We were going somewhere on a mild early September morning, still moist with dew, under cloudless skies.

In the office parking lot, I found the best compromise between shade and proximity to weeds where you could urinate. As soon as possible, I examined my morning schedule and had the office staff reschedule the patients at the end of the morning who I thought could wait until a later date. Then, I introduced you to the two nurses who I thought would be most willing to help you if I became too busy. You were surly to both of them; you frightened one enough that I lost her cooperation; the other, a nurse who owned your sister from the same litter until she died two years earlier, had a softer spot in her heart for you and attributed your behavior to your condition. But you made it clear that I would need to take you for your mini-walks throughout the morning. I probably required the regular reassurance of these walks that your suffering did not end prematurely as the September sun moved higher in the sky and heated the van.

I still had to make arrangements with your veterinarian to treat you later that day after I completed my morning of patients. By the time I arrived at my office, it was late enough that I no longer feared getting the recording that previously increased my desperation by directing me to an emergency room. Not only did I reach a live human voice, but it also expressed concern and it did not hesitate to allow me to speak directly to your local vet. This warm reception contrasted with the one in my own office where the reception staff protects their busy physicians during office hours from patient phone calls. I was prepared for this kind of reception, but was gratified that something in your ordeal finally went silky smooth.

We were able to agree on a time for the appointment. I

volunteered to find a Foley catheter for you; she would locate the dye necessary to do the x-ray study of your bladder. When I failed to find an appropriately gauged catheter in the South Haven Emergency room, the nurse who raised your late sister took up your cause and eventually located a small pediatric catheter that would slide past the bone in your penis. This catheter never would leave my desk because the urethra, the channel inside the penis, of a large dog is over twice as long as the urethra of a small child. Nevertheless, her compassionate act during this bleak period was a welcome break in the clouds.

    I somehow cobbled a morning of empathetic patient care with taking you for frequent walks and recounting your plight to anyone who might listen. My co-workers seemed genuinely concerned about you, most likely out of concern for me. For my part, I felt slightly embarrassed to be so overwrought about a dog. Izzy, do not take this personally. We humans place a higher value on human life than that of any other animal, even though we treat our dogs, in many cases, better than most humans and we treat humans like dogs. We appreciate the simplicity and predictability of canine loyalty and unconditional love over the complexity and unpredictability of human relationships. But it is the duplicitous human created in the image of God endowed with reason and consciousness who we hold most sacred. He who seems to value Canine Familiaris over Homo sapiens at any time must, therefore, be a tad pathetic and a lower form of human. But on that morning, I was working among a group of people who had, over the years, become my work family and did not seem to judge the source of my human anguish.

    My morning of juggling your needs with patient care mercifully was winding down. I had finished seeing patients. I dashed off responses to patient phone messages and gathered the charts of patients that I would need to dictate later. Your veterinarian called around this time to make final arrangements for our rendezvous in a couple of hours. When she inquired, I told her about your uneventful morning and the catheter I found. We spoke for no more than five minutes, but it was enough to quench my smoldering desperation. Towards the end of this call, one my receptionists came to my work area and informed me that my wife was on the phone about an emergency.

The conversation was about to conclude, so I thanked your local vet again. But my mind leaped right away to all sorts of scenarios, having to do with Cindy's aging parents or my recently widowed mother or some unforeseen tragic event at school where my wife taught. Everything that could have been done with you had been done, so I did not consider that you had anything to do with her emergency. I was alarmed but I had no idea what disaster she had to impart. My mind flew to many, but no single one, and did not even consider the right one.

I hit the private line. "Hi Cindy," I said cautiously.

"I can't find him anywhere. I've looked all over, and I can't find Izzy anywhere." Cindy was sobbing on the other end.

"Cindy. He's fine. He's with me in the back of the van. He's OK. I didn't tell you because I didn't think I could get it all together, and when I did, I did everything I needed to do except tell you. Cindy, I'm so sorry."

Her grief still gushed from her like she had not heard me. "I looked everywhere. I came home during lunch to see how he was doing. I thought we decided to leave him outside and he wasn't there. When he wasn't on the front porch, I looked all over the inside of the house." Thinking about it started a new round of sobs before she continued. "He wasn't there. Then I looked around the pond. I thought I might find him floating. And then I walked all the way down to the creek. I kept calling him and calling him and he didn't come." She tried to catch her breath. "When he didn't come, I thought I was going to find him… dead." And she convulsed with sobs again.

"Cindy, I'm so sorry. He's fine. I thought he would be more comfortable in the back of the van."

She choked, "I thought that I was going to find him…."

"I'm so sorry, Cindy. I'm soooooo sorry. It's my fault. I should have told you."

If I had any lingering doubt about how much you meant to Cindy until then, her flood of grief at that moment dispelled it. Her imagination could not bear the thought that you had wandered off and died somewhere in the acres of woods behind our house. Until then, I believed that I was the only one who loved your unruly nature unconditionally and would have experienced such a depth of emotion over the imagined scenario. The terror and sorrow in her voice did not subside for several minutes, even after my assurances about your whereabouts and my non-stop apologies. Her terror and sorrow burrowed through me and generated a river of remorse. Just when I was beginning to feel comfortable about your treatment, I was responsible for filling the other important human being in your life with terror. If only I had left a note. At the time, my actions seemed unforgivable. I thought that I had traumatized her for life. Perhaps, she was right that my benign negligence and my chronic habit of benign tardiness amounted to gross inconsiderateness. I did not try to excuse my negligence because I only wanted her to rebound to the state of hopefulness to which my morning's activity had brought me. I know now that I did not write the note, because I did not know for sure that I was going to put you in the back of the van until I closed the door behind you.

By that time, the engine was running and I was down the driveway. At that moment, your needs were more important than my own, and apparently Cindy's.

****

Cindy did eventually calm down and agreed to meet you and me at the veterinarian's office that afternoon. We arrived nearly simultaneously at the office a few minutes before your appointment. While we waited for your veterinarian, we walked you around the building so that you could go through the motions of leaving your scent on the young, low shrubs. You looked good and you seemed happy walking around with us under sparkling afternoon skies. It was an ideal day to take you down to the beach where your joy could infect me and heal me. As I walked you through the corridor into the wide-open waiting area, I thought that it had to be obvious to anyone watching that a healthy, handsome, majestic, grizzled beast like you was worth any effort to save. In a short time, your veterinarian arrived. She explained later that she kept us waiting a few minutes because she herself had to retrieve the contrast material necessary for your x-ray.

From the outset, our experience in the veterinarian's office contrasted favorably with that in the city animal hospital. We received the same warm welcome, just not as saccharine. After we discussed your situation briefly in the waiting room, you were not whisked away to the back room. She recognized that Cindy and I were part of your caring team, like parents for a small child. She treated me like a fellow professional who could remain detached when his pet underwent a potentially traumatizing procedure. She recognized that you might find our presence reassuring during the catheterization procedure. Still, I had been conditioned by my previous experience in the hospital, so I was surprised when she invited us back into the procedure area.

Your veterinarian, rarely one for small-talk, assembled the personnel she needed, her assistant and associate veterinarian, the one who had advised us before we went to hospital days earlier. Then she got right down to business. She had already gathered all the supplies that she would need for the procedure: a 23 inch red rubber tube, a large blue plastic basin capable of holding over a gallon, a 2 ounce syringe, gloves, towels and a muzzle for you. As you had always found the muzzle emasculating, I put it on your snout myself to show you that I approved of the procedure to follow. Until then, I had wondered how they ever lifted your 100 pounds up on the table in the hospital, because every time I tried to lift your front legs or your back legs into the car or van, you yelped and I desisted. However, what was a mystery to me was second nature to the staff. Your vet grasped your chest behind the front legs while I grasped your pelvis in front of the hind legs. We had just arrived and already you were up on the stainless steel table on your left side, confused, but not rebelling.

Next, we learned the magical procedure that became your lifeline for the rest of your days. If we added this ability to our repertoire, we believed that we could keep you alive indefinitely. Unsheathing your raw, beefy penis that always seemed slightly obscene to me, like a leering little old man's, was reduced to pure sleight of hand. If muzzling you was humiliating, what must it have been for you to have your procreating organ and the conduit of your male prowess manipulated like Fila dough? Yet, in your vet's experienced hands, you surrendered peacefully. Later I would learn that you had muscles to retract the penis into its shell like the head of a threatened turtle, but you did not use them then. Your shaved pink soft hindquarters, a remnant of your stay in the

Kalamazoo, made the appearance of your penis all that much more dramatic.

The procedure was really quite simple, requiring more guts than it did skill. Your vet stabilized your penis with her left hand by grabbing the back of the penile bone beneath the skin of your soft, pink shaved underbelly. While pushing forward on the bone with her left hand, she slipped the prepuce, or foreskin, back with her right hand. Your beefy penis arose in all of its glory. She then held the foreskin back with her right hand until the left hand could replace it, both stabilizing the penis and holding the foreskin back with one hand. This freed her right hand to thread the lubricated tip of the catheter into the small, flaccid opening of your penis and slide it forward until urine burbled out of the other end.

She then attached the syringe to the open end of the catheter and while the other veterinarian gently applied pressure over your bladder, she filled and drained the syringe 40 times, removing more than half a gallon of urine from your bladder. Your normal bladder capacity was about a pint. Only then did I understand the magnitude of your problem and discomfort. Your bladder, for some still unknown reason had expanded to more than five times its normal capacity. Instead of an expanding and contracting orange, I imagined an empty, floppy water bottle inside of you. How would it ever regain it former shape, size, strength, and function?

Your vet allowed me to practice the maneuver of coaxing your penis from the foreskin before taking you back for your x-ray procedure. For our own protection from radiation, your vet did not invite us into the x-ray suite. The procedure went quickly, however, and you were placed back in our care, muzzle-free and pain-free. You seemed happy and grateful and I thought I detected an attitude of understanding about the necessity of all you had undergone. Your vet took us back to the dark room where we could view your x-ray films. She showed us that your urethra, the drainage tube in your penis, was unobstructed and had a normal diameter except for a little expected narrowing through the prostate. Your bladder, while large, seemed to have a smooth contour and was free of stones and growths in the wall. There was no obvious explanation for why your bladder had grown to five times its normal size and would not empty normally.

A theory was beginning to emerge, however, in light of the absence of an obstruction, stones, and evidence for neurologic damage to your hindquarters. What if your legendary bladder capacity up in Suttons Bay was the beginning of your enlarging bladder? A few weeks earlier, you had exhausted yourself diving for boulders and chasing geese. You were unable to stop yourself and I did not have the heart to cage you inside the house; life for you was becoming too short. By evening, when you were done begging for scraps from our late dinners, you collapsed on the navy blue room rug in the living room, dead to the world. Most nights, it was difficult enough to get you to stand on all four feet and make you walk the twenty-foot hallway to our bedroom; it seemed inconceivable to make you walk an additional 75 feet, including a few stair steps, to go outside to urinate. I also expected that you would have let me know if that were necessary, either by barking or having an accident inside. Neither occurred.

Might your bladder have accommodated your exhausted body? On top of these long stretches in which you did not urinate, you had been for over a year an inveterate water drinker. We were beginning to surmise that your problem with urinating might not have begun as suddenly as it seemed, on that one awful day and evening five days earlier. Cindy and I did not study the strength of your stream every time you urinated and we did not keep track of whether the urine you eliminated approximated the amount that you ingested. We assumed that every time you lifted your leg or squatted (as you did more often in your latter years), you left your mark in the usual abundance. Those sorts of things were supposed to take care of themselves.

The theory seemed plausible. Your obsession with boulders and our negligence of your need to empty your bladder in combination with your excessive drinking had caused your bladder problem. Your veterinarian had not only given you relief; she had made it possible to arrive at a possible diagnosis. She had accomplished this in 5% of the time that the staff had in hospital and at half the cost, performing the test in an afternoon that hospital could not arrange in 60 hours.

What's more, in consultation with a veterinarian internist on the other side of the state, she had arrived at a rational treatment plan for you. It was imperative, the consultant believed, to keep the bladder as empty as possible so that it could regain its integrity. He had recommended that we place an indwelling catheter in you for 30 days in the hospital. For all we knew, thirty days could amount to half of your remaining life; no quality and no way. Alternatively, we could catheterize you at home two to three times a day, preferably every six to eight hours. That was the only practical alternative; both Cindy and I were prepared to do whatever it took to give you the greatest quality of life.

Additionally, your local vet recommended a couple of medications. One medication would relax the muscles at the floor of your bladder to reduce the resistance your bladder had to overcome. This medication, manufactured only for humans to treat hypertension associated with a rare condition called pheochromocytoma, was rarely used. When I looked into it later on, I discovered that it had many side effects and that a month's worth of treatment would cost $1000 dollars. I decided to look into other human medicines that did the same thing with fewer side effects and that were much more readily available. The other medicine that she recommended, at that time, would strengthen the muscle contractions of your bladder wall. We were to hold off on that one until she received confirmation from the radiologist that there was no obstruction on the x-ray in your urinary tract.

Finally, she was concerned about the amount of water that you were drinking. She agreed with Cindy that we should closely monitor your water intake. In the short term, that meant that we could not take you to Lake Michigan to dive for rocks or let you outside in our yard unmonitored, because you might gorge yourself at the pond. She suggested that we limit your daily water to 2 quarts, the calculated requirement for your weight. So as much as I believed your ordeal had earned you a trip to the beach and as much as the mild, clear day beckoned us to a calm, rocky shoreline, I had to submit to the less impaired judgment of your veterinarian and Cindy. Where were Aunt Norma and her belief in the restorative powers of water when I needed them?

Your vet also gave us a bag of departing gifts that would remain useful for the rest of your life. It included a bundle of 23 inch red rubber catheters like the one she had used earlier that day, two large syringes, a large blue basin like the one she had used earlier, and a bottle of concentrated sterilizing solution. My office would provide all the other supplies for your catheterization—sterile lubricating gel for the tip of the catheter, gloves, and absorptive chucks. Your vet alleviated my greatest concern in her departing tips on catheterizing you. All along I had believed that it would be necessary to lift you onto a raised surface that simulated the procedure table, like a picnic table, to properly catheterize you. While I had few concerns about myself, I was concerned that the fifty-pound half left to Cindy would bring back her sciatica in no time, not to mention the toll on your already painful hips and elbows. I felt silly about these concerns when she told us that we could catheterize you lying on the ground, and that, weather permitting, we could do it outside in the grass if we wanted. That way, we would not have to worry about urine soaking the floor or carpet. When we left, my only remaining concern was that our unkempt yard would create a field of obstructing blades of grass when I came to the most delicate part of the procedure.

****

We never did catheterize you in the grass, though we may have tried once before we recognized its folly. We started out on the back porch among the flitting moths where we spent the long night before going to the Kalamazoo animal hospital. After a few days, we moved the procedure indoors in front of the sofa in the living room. Your operating suite was the coziest in all of southwest Michigan—on the southwestern wall, 12 feet of floor to ceiling picture windows overlooking a mature forest of beech, oak, maple, and hemlock in our backyard; on the northwestern wall a see-through fireplace and hearth of river stone overlooked by a large tapestry of a wide-eyed owl pieced together of earth-toned llama hides; and three spotlights, two in the ceiling focused on the hearth, providing general light for the suite, and an extra lamp, that focused on your procedure. You were frequently there already, sound asleep, and we could continue to watch or listen to the television beside the hearth, if we wanted. Eventually we honed the procedure sufficiently that we could have done it anywhere in the house where there was enough light, but as we kept most of the supplies on the hearth in the living room, catheterizing you in the living room became as routine and natural as it was to brush our teeth in the bathroom. While it may not seem possible that a procedure so invasive, humiliating, and unnatural could evolve to such a degree, Cindy and I willed the process to become part of our lives, rather than a disruption in it.

We had ample opportunity to improve the efficiency of the procedure, doing it three times a day for the first couple of weeks. For the most part, Cindy allowed me to take charge of the procedure, because of my medical training and because it worked better to have one master chef in the kitchen. She assumed a supportive role so well that we functioned more as a single unit rather than a leader and a subordinate. She made and took suggestions in a way that created little friction, born of her love for you and for me, subordinating a natural tendency to take control like she would in her classroom. Additionally, in order to meet the catheterization schedule, even while starting out a new school year, she cut her sleep at the margins to assist with early morning and late night catheterizations. She was my third and forth hand, an extra lobe in my cortex, and a flow of calming endorphins and GABA neurotransmitters in my brain. In our drive to make you comfortable, we, humans and canine, became a trinity of heroes, functioning at the positive margins of our capabilities.

Constantly, if not obsessively aware of your needs, I usually determined the schedule of these catheterizations. Since the goal was to shrink your bladder, I tried to space them so that your bladder would not overfill. Not only was I aware of when your last catheterization was, but I also tried to track the patterns of your urine production, when and how much water you were drinking, and how much urine you were eliminating naturally. When I decided that it was time to catheterize you, I would usually give Cindy a three to five minute warning. During that interval, I retrieved one of several red rubber catheters soaking in a pan of dilute Betadine in the kitchen and wiped it down with isopropyl alcohol. Holding it by its funneled open end, I took it into the adjacent living room where you were frequently visible through the see-through fireplace, and laid it on a bed of clean paper towels that I had prepared for it. From a box of supplies on the hearth, I retrieved k-y jelly and a 2 ounce syringe, squirting a dab of jelly on the paper towel and laying the syringe beside it. Then I usually called for Cindy. You were usually already nearby and sometimes already in position. At first, I thought that the catheter struck a fearful chord in your heart and tried to shield your view of it, but eventually, it appeared that you developed an attitude of tolerance, acceptance, and even gratitude toward it. When Cindy arrived in the room, one of us put the muzzle on you. We tried to share that responsibility, at first, because it was more humiliating and punishing in some ways than the catheterization procedure itself.

After placing the muzzle on you, in time, you usually knew what was to follow. A two-person job at first, Cindy easily maneuvered you by herself to your left side on the carpet with your legs resting in front of you. You had to be on your left so that I could thread the catheter with my right hand and hold the penis with my left; I was not adept enough to do it the other way around. Sometime between preparing the catheter and laying you down, I commenced what I considered the biggest bane of the whole procedure. I started to glove. So many times, to the point of becoming ludicrous, I said to Cindy, "I have to solve the glove problem," and then would not change a thing. Every other step in the procedure, we worked out to save time and reduce tension. In her supportive role, Cindy's attention could not drift during the many steps of the procedure, and if ever it did and there was a brief hitch in the process, she quickly apologized; in the heat of the moment, it all seemed so vital—vital to minimize the time spent with the disease and to maximize time spent enjoying life.

But I could not solve the gloving problem. I believed at first that I had to glove like I would for any human procedure each time I catheterized you to prevent infection in your bladder. As I had no idea if I would need to do it for months or years to come, I felt that I had to conserve on the number of gloves I used for environmental and financial reasons. As my hands were visible in my work and my hands broke out in an itchy, grotesque rash if I did not use hypoallergenic gloves, I was forced to use pre-packaged hypoallergenic gloves from my office. I decided to reuse the gloves. At first, I rinsed them after each use and hung them on the back of porch chairs to dry; it took days for each pair to dry, so I had a half dozen pairs going at a time. When this method became too cumbersome, I decided to use an inexpensive disposable glove over the hypoallergenic glove so that the hypoallergenic glove would be in contact with my hand and the inexpensive glove would absorb the contamination from urine. This was the method I used until the last week.

My prepackaged gloves, however, had two distinct sides—one was smooth and slid easily over my hands and the other was relatively tacky to enhance the grip during procedures. When removing the gloves after each use, whatever side was in would turn out and visa versa. As a consequence, I struggled to put the glove on my hand when the tacky side was in or struggled with the overglove if it was out. I had to tug repeatedly on each bunched finger of each glove like a stocking on a wet foot, usually with partial success; I pulled and it would snap back, and then I pulled again and again. When my frustration reached its limit and I had to proceed, I was usually wearing a cross between a glove and a mitten. The ordeal was not only frustrating, but it ultimately reduced the sensitivity of my grip when manipulating your delicate parts and threading the eye of your needle.

I got my hands back when I decided in what turned-out to be your last week to stop wearing gloves. Cindy had stopped wearing gloves weeks earlier, but I felt that since I was manipulating the part of the catheter that ended up in your bladder, I had to wear a clean pair of gloves. I was never concerned about contaminating my own hands as I have an abiding faith in my own immune system and the cleansing effect of soap and water. By the time I stopped wearing gloves, a germ with a nauseating fecal odor had already colonized your urine and you had bigger problems than a few extra germs from my hands. During that week, I understood the opportunity I missed to make your life and my life easier. Compared to my gloved technique, barehanded I was able to expose more and stabilize more securely while giving you relief. Little things like this and knowing right where my magnifying glasses were seemed like major things during these rarified six weeks.

Your behavior during the catheterizations was the most heroic and hopeful. Had you put up a struggle with any stage of the procedure or shown significant suffering, I do not think that Cindy and I could have continued with your care. From the outset, you never hid or headed the other direction when you noticed me setting up for the procedure. When we brought you to the living room, you did not plant your feet at any point. When we pulled the muzzle from the supply box on the hearth and headed in your direction, you did not turn your head from side to side like a two-year-old who hates getting his face washed. When it was time to lay you on your left side, you nearly put yourself in the proper position. When it came time to bare your conduit of your alpha male scent, you relaxed your muscles enough that I felt like a pro most times at a procedure at which I was really an amateur.

You resisted only when I was probably hurting you, retracting your penis into its sheath at a time I was already having a particularly difficult time unhooding it. Only then did you wince and lift you muzzled snout pleadingly in my direction. Cindy, who was usually focused on the procedure, would then divert her attention to comforting you by stroking your neck and offering soothing words to your deaf ears. If I had to suppress on a regular basis the gut-wrenching feeling that I had at these times, I would have approached each catheterization with trepidation and diffidence. For most of the six weeks, you had the strength and will to submit. You submitted, not because you were overpowered, but because you sensed our love and you trusted us. When we completed the procedure and removed the muzzle, you rebounded and accepted our biscuit with your usual zest, allaying our guilt. For that small act, I have the greatest gratitude.

I kept a running record of the results of all your catheterizations. In addition to keeping track of the frequency and amount of urine from your catheterizations, I believed that the record might chart your progress and provide helpful information for your veterinarian. I used chemistry urine dipsticks from the doctor's office regularly to determine the concentration, or specific gravity, of your urine and to detect blood and white blood cells, signs of infection. The information might eventually help us determine whether you had a disorder that made it impossible for you to concentrate your urine, causing you to drink large amounts of water. If we found evidence for this disorder, a medication was available to concentrate your urine and prevent the excessive consumption of water.

I did not miss a single recording during the six-week period. The paperwork became, in a way, sacred to me, symbolic of our efforts to keep you among us. I tried to minimize the ripple that the paper gradually acquired from my hands, still damp from measuring your urine, washing the basin, and rinsing the syringe. My last recording was at the very bottom of the backside of the page. I had no idea that the rest of your life would fit on the front and back of a single sheet of paper.

****

We had our first opportunity to catheterize you the day after your catheterization at the veterinarian's office. Though we had limited your water intake and access to the pond down the road, we still withdrew four to five times your normal bladder capacity, filling and emptying the 2-ounce syringe almost 35 times, Cindy kneading your abdomen over your bladder while I worked the syringe. After the first day, a Friday, we had the weekend to get into the habit of catheterizing you three times daily. Never again did we remove more than a quart of urine from your bladder during any single catheterization, and most times, we drained an amount that was near or below your normal bladder capacity. The amounts gradually diminished until they leveled off at just over a quart total spread out through the three daily catheterizations. Finally, after filling the syringe only once during an entire 24 period, we stopped catheterizing you completely for up to two or three days at a time.

Limiting your water seemed to help your problem, but the introduction of medications, one in particular, seemed to help you even more. From the time we started the catheterizations, I gave you some sort of antibiotic to prevent or treat urinary tract infections, though I was never sure that antibiotics made a difference. We also introduced a couple medications that affected the muscles involved with urination. One was a human medicine called Flomax that reduced the muscular resistance that the bladder had to overcome. I spent hours on the Internet trying to reassure myself that it would work for you and could be given safely. However, I began using the medicine after your veterinarian discussed its use with one of her old professors at Michigan State, who gave his approval based upon several decades of experience, not research.

During this same discussion, he recommended treating your excessive drive to drink water with a medication that concentrated urine, DDAVP or Desmopressin. This medication had three forms, a nasal spray, injection, and tablets. The tablets were the most expensive and were absorbed unreliably from the gut. The nasal spray seemed less invasive than the injection, so we tried it first. However, you were not very receptive to a spray into the most sensitive, most powerful sensory organ still available to you. I was forced to tiptoe stealthily upon you while you were sleeping. Sometimes, you woke up before I could angle the spray bottle properly, and when you saw the bottle, instantly started batting your head from side to side like a two year old getting his face washed. Other times, if you did not wake up, the finicky spray bottle misfired in a way that left me unsure if the spray went in your nose. When the spray did enter your nose, it was obvious because you would awaken instantly from any level of sleep and smack your lips like you bit into a sour lime. Only when I started injecting the same medication into a big pinch of skin did you get the medication reliably and your urine production dropped off precipitously.

The final medication we used stimulated your bladder muscle to work. Overall, I was never sure that any of the medications made a difference with the exception of the one the decreased your urine production. Still I used all of them when you were doing well, and withdrew some or all of them when something seemed to sap all your strength in the last week, when you were dying right before my eyes.

****

Cindy and I were not averse to catheterizing you for years to come if you still had some quality of life. If necessary, we planned to take you with us to Nova Scotia the following summer with your portable supplies, a catheter, basin and syringe, and your medications. However, our goal was to wean your from the catheter by shrinking your bladder and re-establishing its function. Not only did we catheterize you regularly and limit your water, but we also made sure that you had frequent and regular opportunities to urinate, every two or three hours while you were awake. This was not difficult on weekends or during the evening, but during the week, we both had regular jobs that threatened to undo everything by allowing your bladder to overfill. Fortunately, Cindy and I worked close enough to home that each of us could race home over our lunch break for a visit and take you out. We had plenty to do during our brief lunch breaks, but you had moved to the center of our lives and become our labor of love. I usually arrived home first, and would leave a daily note for Cindy about your efforts. "Izzy seems to be feeling better. Spent some time lying in the sunshine with him while I dictated a couple charts. Trickle followed by a squirt," or "Urinated with good stream three times. Hope your day is going as well. Love, David"

During the first two weeks, you went through the motions as if nothing was wrong, sometimes lifting your leg, but usually squatting like a female unless you assumed a position halfway between defecation and urination to apply all you might to emptying your bladder. To allay my frustration and also to quantify your progress, I would count the seconds in my head, one one-thousand, two one-thousand, etc. until I saw the first drop of urine. Sometimes you struck a pose for twenty-five or thirty seconds before I stopped counting. After some time, a dribble came, followed by a succession of large raindrops, and usually as you were walking away, a sustained squirt. If I had time, I walked you up and down our quarter mile gravel road in the hope that your stream would improve with practice or that the cumulative volume of your squirts would make a difference. I took advantage of your alpha male instincts by walking you around our neighbor's yard halfway down the road. Whether the scent of their dog increased the volume of your urination overall is unclear, but it certainly increased your level of animation and your overall attempts. In those first couple weeks, you did not have a stream, but your squirts became more frequent with the proper motivation, and more sustained. I was heartened by the mere suggestion of improvement.

    When I reported your first stream to Cindy, I believed it was a fluke, like a baby turning over by accident months before he does it purposely; you had dribbled and squirted for two weeks without any significant improvement. It seemed if you were going to have a stream, there should have been steady progress toward it. An infant does not suddenly walk one day; he usually crawls, cruises along furniture and stands up unassisted briefly before he takes his first steps. But in your case, it was not a fluke or an accident. Your stream continued, on command; my counting did not get past three seconds. It appeared that if we kept your urine volume below a certain level, your bladder functioned, and once it rose above that level, your stream began to deteriorate.

    My joy watching you urinate freely exceeded that of watching a child take his first steps. We expect children to reach this milestone. I had no idea if you would ever have a stream again. It was a small miracle. When the sunshine caught your stream, it was like watching a ribbon of liquid gold. What bliss the sick gave to the healer, the dog to the human!

I shared our good news with your veterinarian, because I wanted her to know that her efforts to formulate a plan on your behalf had worked; Cindy and I had provided care that would have overwhelmed most pet owners, but I felt like we labored to fulfill her plan. Not that I was without a sense of triumph, but it was tempered by the remaining facts: you were still a dog in the final months or years of your life that was deaf and fragile and required four medications. Still I spoke of our success out loud because I could not foresee any reason why you would ever again lose your bladder function. As long as we did our part, your problem should not return.

As a founding member of the killjoy club who usually tried to see the big picture, had I believed our success as only temporary, I would not have claimed it aloud. I continued to hawk your urine stream for subtle changes that might signal a need to catheterize you. Entire days went by when I did not count past three seconds before I reveled in your steady stream; I began counting how long your stream lasted instead of how long it took to start it. Sometimes, you had a series of streams, the second stronger than the first. My heart pranced with you as you paraded around your old territory, reclaiming it with a steady stream of liquid gold. During these days, I soared with you. One must understand the height of my joy to recognize the depth of my disappointment when a couple weeks later we returned to square one with your urinary stream.

****

Though a slice of my heart helplessly followed the bouncing ball of your urinary stream, we had intended to make your bladder maintenance as routine as possible so that, for the remainder of your life, we could focus on the activities that gave you pleasure and joy. By this time, the formula for your joy was simple. You had given up power walks with us months earlier; you lost the strength to explore the woods for a new canine scent in the neighborhood; your deafness to the arrival of our neighbors next door silenced your obnoxious bark and ended your harassing forays; and the turning over of an engine next door was no longer an invitation to indulge your obsession for the rotating whitewalls for which you saved your most ferocious growl. You were also deaf to the movement of the refrigerator door that used to bring you to the kitchen from anywhere in the house to bum a scrap. The nip of your worn teeth no longer greeted visitors. You lost the drive and the power in your hind legs to hump strangers and the members of your human family, like our sons, whom you deemed lower in the den hierarchy. You lost the stamina to stand, drool, beg, and ruin our evening meals with your puppy dog eyes. You outright lost the energy that you required to misbehave. We could finally indulge many of your bad habits and all of your good ones without the disturbing consequences that they had most of your life.

You derived most of your pleasure from food, bodies of water, diving for rocks, riding in cars, and just being with us. Your behavior alone would have confirmed the theory that dog behavior evolved as a means to manipulate humans to provide them with food, giving dogs a survival advantage over their chump ancestors who had to hunt and scavenge for theirs. In our family, I was the most susceptible to your charms and subtle and not-so-subtle harassment. I maintained that if I consistently shared bits of my food with you, I would deflect your inevitable obnoxious behaviors from others. Usually, I would save the last little bit of whatever I was eating to share with you (though occasionally I would slip a little something under the table in the middle of the meal and risk a scolding). I rarely offered you the dregs but a chunk that I would have consumed myself had you not been there, a piece of beef, not a piece of fat that I would have tossed myself. I gave you a prime corner of peanut butter toast, not just a burnt piece of crust. When I finished my dinner, frequently in the face of Cindy's protest, I gave you my plate with a solid scrap to scarf down before you licked it spotless. You were the best pre-wash for dishes that a dishwasher could have.

The only meal remnant that I gave you that I really did not want was the milk at the bottom of my cereal bowl. This became your favorite, and was one of the events around which you organized your morning. You impatiently waited for me to finish my morning stretching exercises, a preparatory prelude to the day for me, but for you, an unwanted interlude before your morning milk. Sunday morning, you had to settle for oatmeal mixed in with your milk. Otherwise, I only gave you food that I wanted myself; that was appropriate for my canine brother, son, companion, and alter ego.

I not only regularly whet your appetite for human food, but also showered you with dog biscuits, usually before I departed the house. I used the biscuit as a transitional vehicle—my apology for leaving and your reward for staying and guarding the house. I would announce my departure with the three words that meant "biscuit" to you, "Guard the house." Eventually, you became so intensely aware of my various departure routines, I told Cindy, "He knows I am leaving before I do sometimes." I would find you staring me down when I was immersed in my morning routine and for a second, I could not fathom what was on your mind. Then it would hit me, "You know that I am leaving and I have not given you a biscuit." Sometimes, I could not get out of the house without giving you most of three large biscuits. If ever I hesitated to leave, while gathering my patient charts, looking for a pen, finding my gloves, changing a book on tape, whatever, your fixated eyes demanded an encore as successfully as a raucous standing ovation. I found that look so humorous, so stereotypically you, I never minded giving in to it, no matter how rushed I was. I suppose you carried five extra pounds all your life because of that look. If not for the weight gain, I would have bought stock in a dog biscuit company.

Cindy thought I was wasting food on you and seriously contributing to your delinquent behavior, that is, until the end. If I did not successfully hide my pandering from her, she laced the pleasure I took in sharing my food with you with guilt. But part of the beauty of recognizing the beginning of your end was that we viewed you with a single set of eyes and a single heart. We both derived pleasure in giving you the final half-inch of milk at the bottom of our bowls and the residue of our plates; there was no waste if by sharing our meals with you, we let you know that we were also sharing our lives with you.

We humans are capable only of human emotions. Usually we express our affection or contempt toward other humans, but what if the object of our affection is a faithful dog that loves and adores us unconditionally, like few humans ever have? Do we have a unique sort of love for an animal, or is the feeling going to be a variant of the love we express for other humans? At a fundamental level, we experience a dog as a companion, a family member, and our alter ego, vulnerable on one hand and quite capable of protecting us on the other. We feel a non-carnal love for our pet that is distinctly human and that is a unique hodgepodge of love for all these entities. We will not have a canine emotion because it is a canine that we happen to love. So for those of you who wish to minimize the loss of a pet by saying, "It is only a dog," I must answer, "I am only a human."

Not once during your final six weeks did we take your presence for granted. Our spontaneous need to care for you flowed straight from the heart, like a parent's vigilant sixth sense for his toddler at play combined with an adult child's concern for his fragile elderly parent. Like the toddler, we needed to know where you were at all times, but like an elderly parent, we knew your habits and usually where to find you. We took comfort in knowing you were where you were supposed to be, even in your deaf, profoundly exhausted state. When we readied ourselves each morning in front of our large bathroom mirror, you lay nearby between the bed and the file cabinets in our adjacent bedroom with your back to the bathroom door, waiting for me to head down the hall toward the coat rack in the dining room where I kept all my ties. Your whereabouts penetrated my consciousness like the refrain of an unending song. At times, I would walk to the door of the bathroom to assure myself of your presence. Toward the end, you were often sprawled out on your side, but on your good days, you sat on your belly like a blond sphinx with your hind legs beneath you and your front legs stretched in front—in your world of silence in a pose of uncharacteristic patience. Sitting there, you were more than a piece of furniture; you were for me better than Prozac, valium, and a massage rolled into one.

You did have healthier pursuits than consuming food. During the latter weeks and months of your life, one of your loves coincided with one of ours—going to the beach. There you scavenged for your boulders and we searched for our beautiful pebbles and stones. For a short time, we had to put our mutual pursuit on hold until we could reign in your urge to consume the lake while diving in it. Cindy, as usual, was the enforcer here, until we received permission from the vet to head down to the beach again. You must thank Cindy some day for this hiatus, because I would have killed you sooner with all my love and concern.

Cindy and I had complementing strengths that would eventually converge. I knew that just climbing into the van and anticipating the beach breathed new life in you like watering a limp plant. We both needed the beach, the waves, the boulders, and sand. I was nagged by what percentage each non-beach day might be of the remainder of your life. We held out for an entire week before we received the go-ahead to rock hound. On your urination diary that day, I remarked, "Dove for rocks." You had not lost or forgotten a thing.

Izzy, you were inextricably bound to our rediscovery of the beaches around South Haven. Your need to cool off in the lake water was already the reason we wove down the pallet-covered path from Evergreen Bluff. Before that, I enjoyed what I believed was the best view of the winding shoreline of South Haven from some forty feet up on Evergreen Bluff, while looking south toward the lighthouse at the mouth of the Black River. But your passion ignited ours. Traversing the slatted pallets that covered the boggy path to the beach should have been treacherous for you, but the water ahead infused you with the agility of a younger dog. Reinvigorated by your sorties into the lake, you then ran up the path unscathed. Among the large boulders and broken concrete slabs strewn on the beach during earlier times to protect the bluff, your human companions began to find the patterned stones, at first, flat brown stones broken by stellate white streaks called "lightning stones". I found that from the beach it was nearly as beautiful to look east, away from the lake, up the steep bluff through the spray of green brush and scrubby trees, alive with flitting redwing blackbirds, into a deepening blue late afternoon sky.

The time would come, however, when we ended our

longer walks with you, and we stopped going to this section of the beach. We still made the walk to Evergreen Bluff without you, but never went down to the beach. When we encountered the residents of that street who had gotten to know us over a decade as a threesome, some assumed the worst about you and, out of consideration for us, did not ask about your whereabouts. But others would stop and ask, and were relieved to learn that you were at home resting your achy joints.

During the final six weeks, we drove only to the beach. Mainly, we went to the beach at the end of Deerlick Street, where the Deerlick Creek that wound along the southwestern border of our property eventually emptied into Lake Michigan less than a mile away. But we explored other beaches nearby along Lake Michigan to see what different stony treasures the waves had deposited.

A patient of mine piqued our interest in a beach 15 miles north of us when she brought in a couple of rocks as a gift, a lightning stone and a small geode. She had no idea that we were born-again rock hounds and was surprised by my unabashed delight in her gift. She lived in Glenn, Michigan, and she told me that the rocks were so deep along the shore where she lived that the Department of Natural Resources measured the depth of the rocks there to gage the depth along the entire shoreline. When the rocks were "out", not swallowed up by the sand, she led me to believe that she lived in rock heaven. She invited us to the beach in her back yard, but instead we made the fifteen-mile trip north to a beach nearby at the West Side County Park, a public park just north of Glenn, Michigan.

Other times, we went to a beach a half-mile south of Deerlick at the bottom of a dead end street girded with "No Parking" signs. But Cindy had done her research and knew that it was a public access. Here, a shifting shallow stream carved the beach enough to unearth a few boulders that entertained you when you became too weak to withstand the force of the Lake Michigan. Finally, if the sunset was near or just past, we headed to the large open South Beach near the pier and lighthouse. There were no boulders or stones, but you did not seem to mind wandering the gentle slope of the large sugar-sand beach in the dimming light while Cindy took long-exposure photographs of the evolving sunset.

****

We were never deterred by the prospect of inclement weather, instead perceiving it as an opportunity to have the beach to ourselves. We especially liked the mild, gray calm days that looked uninviting, but created perfect conditions along the shoreline, glassy surfaces through which we could see the rocks and benign wavelets for your aching legs. So, when the skies were gray or threatening, though an inveterate, amateur meteorologist, I rarely looked at the radar to find out what might lie ahead. On one of these overcast days, we set out to find the park that we believed was in Glenn, Michigan. We expected that we would find the park near the center of the single-block town, but we had to drive several more miles past farms and large lakefront homes before we encountered an empty parking lot in front of a couple recreation fields. The beach was nowhere in sight, but a road ran west along the fields back to a smaller parking lot set between a bathhouse with bathroom facilities and a small picnic area that overlooked Lake Michigan. Besides our van, there was one other car in the lot that belonged to a family of three that was setting up for a picnic.

The beach was not the easily accessed public beach that I imagined for you. You would have to descend five or six stories of steep weathered wooden steps to get to the beach. The beach itself was deep enough, but it sloped steeply at the shoreline, creating a treacherous drop-off for a frail dog. As we descended with our wash buckets for gathering stones, the wind was already beginning to whip around, but the family seemed unalarmed by the increasingly threatening skies. The stones on the beach were much sparser than I imagined, far from rock heaven. There may have been more rocks just in the water, but the onslaught of waves that took their marching orders from the darkening skies on the western horizon, obscured them. On other beaches, when the rocks washed up in deep piles, I could search the same area for half an hour. On this beach, however, I had to cover a large area, passing dozens of beach houses to see enough variety. The few rocks I found may have seemed more colorful than at Deerlick, but I could not be as discriminating.

You, however, did not seem disappointed. You barked with your usual enthusiasm for me to throw a rock. I soon learned that you found the drop-off and force of the waves intimidating. So, as we headed north up the beach, away from Cindy, I tried to place the stones only a few feet into the turbulence of the foaming surf. But you eventually lost interest because you could not retrieve boulders.

The rain spit at first. I barely acknowledged the skies' efforts, even as it offered up a steady light, wind-driven rain. After all, we had depended upon the threat of rain to give us our empty beach. You and I kept walking north in the hope that I might find my own geode, which I knew to exist on that beach. Periodically, I looked back at Cindy who before long shrunk to a thumbnail in the distance. The rain came harder, but I could still see her in the throes of the hunt. Perhaps, she was looking back at me, relying on my good judgment, but as she was the cautious one, I used her as my gage about when to turn back. So I kept up my hunt, but slowed our progress north.

When the first bolt of lightning seemed to split the difference between Cindy and me, I looked back at her again, and found her still on the beach. I considered it unlikely that a bolt would share the same cubic yard of sand with me. Other bolts followed, closer, with ear splitting and bone-wracking thunder. Did you hear it? Did it penetrate your rain-soaked hide? I looked for you this time; I did not see you at first, but I found you nearby before any alarm set in. I reconsidered my odds of a lightning strike when the third bolt seemed to strike where I had been a minute earlier. With this strike, I imagined the heat of lightning transforming the sand into a glassy shard, creating a real "lightning stone". The rain began to fall harder and to seriously pock the sand. I concluded then that weathering this storm had left the realm of adventure and entered one of folly. Had Cindy been calling us in the square-dance-holler of her youthful days in North Carolina, I doubt we would have heard it over the mounting waves and storm. I turned around to head back to the steps and found the beach completely deserted except for you and me. Cindy had disappeared, and now, I knew we were in trouble.

When I thought that it could not rain any harder, it did, or perhaps the headwind just made it seem so. I took the lead, and periodically looked back to make sure you were surviving the assault. I figured that your physique narrower and closer to the ground would make less of a target to the deluge that threw its full brunt directly into our faces. Once, when I looked back, I caught the image that haunted me for some time to come. You were drenched with your thick blond coat plastered to your skin making it appear that the storm had shrunk you in size. Your eyes had closed to those slits they assumed if we ever raised our hand to you. Your ears were pinned back against your head, probably by the wind, but I was reminded of the few times you felt ashamed after a scolding. You doddered on stiff front legs, almost stymied by the sheets of rain. My powerful fearless dog that would have loped through this wind and rain most of his life was now nearly mastered by it. I felt an immense sense of pathos. I was not sure that you were going to make it back to the steps without collapsing and I considered the impossibility of heaving you over my shoulder and carrying you if I had to. My poor judgment, after all, had gotten you into this mess.

Adjusting my pace to yours, I willed you to follow, making my presence just in front of you a beacon in the storm. I felt wetter than I ever had been in my life leaning into the wind, every five feet saturating my saturated t-shirt and making me feel soaked again. The quarter mile of beach seemed both interminable and infinitesimal; I thought we would never make it and when we finally arrived at the steps, it seemed we had made it in an instant.

We found Cindy part way up the steps under the shelter of a large oak tree. It was impossible to tell whether the storm had let up or whether knowing that the van was only several flights of stairs away, out of the wind and away from the roar of the waves, made it seem so. We were still soaked but already feeling drier in the less horizontal rain. While waiting for the storm to slow, still hoping to hound for more rocks, we lingered in this newfound ease in the shelter of the trees. I worried about you making it up several flights of stairs between the beach and the park, especially after fighting the storm; already you required a rest on the way up the 13 steps from the finished side of our basement of our home. But I need not have worried this time. Some of the hill you ascended in the dune brush and grass beside the steps, the rest on the steps, but once we decided that the weather was not going to break, you made a steady ascent with us without stumbling or resting.

At the top of the steps, we found that the downpour had transformed the shallow basin of the small park into a collection of streams and pools up to our ankles. A potpourri of twigs and leaves that had carpeted the sparse grass beneath mature shade trees flowed in the currents of the fresh flood. The picnickers had long ago given up and our van alone remained in the parking lot. We forded the park to our van. Though you were at least as wet as you were when diving for rocks, there was no purpose in drying you off before you stepped up into the van. Only the benevolent hand of God could have wrung us out before getting into the van. Instead, I turned on the engine and, though still late summer, turned the heat on high to 80 degrees to warm and dry us while we gave the storm several more chances to cease.

While we waited, we basked in the secure aftermath of our harrowing experience and listened to a CD of the Dixie Chicks. The roof of the van transformed the pelting rain from our chief antagonist to a tranquil white noise that insulated us from the cares of the rest of the world. You did not pass out, as I would have expected, but lapped loudly at your soaked hind legs. Cindy and I conferred regularly about whether the rain was letting up and how much longer we should wait. The rain came in waves and teased us. Once, when the rain had let up enough to allow the park flood to subside, I left the van and walked to the edge of the bluff. I looked toward the Wisconsin side of the lake, hoping to find a tattered, tomato-red glow parked on the horizon that suggested sunshine in Wisconsin and augured clearing in Michigan; instead a thick uniform blanket of clouds merged with the arc of the lake. Only our decision to depart would bring back the sunshine. By the time we reached Glenn, the dusk of the storm had already cleared.

Of all that transpired in Glenn on that day, it is the background music of the Dixie Chicks in the van that most successfully conjures it and the era of your prolonged departing. Weeks earlier, I had discovered the hit song on the CD while listening to the top 20 video countdown on a cable channel devoted to Pop culture. The song, "Not Ready to Make Nice," protested the verbal abuse the group received from the most conservative contingent of their fan base after they criticized the policies of George Bush. I was instantly enamored with the song and predicted that it would reach number one, which it did for a record thirteen consecutive weeks.

Cindy surprised me with the entire CD while we were in Suttons Bay when your troubles began to brew. By the time of our rainout in Glenn, I had tired of "Not Ready to Make Nice", but had found several songs in the first six of the CD that I liked just as much, especially the second, "Easy Silence." This was a beautiful, acoustic song that recast the awkward or it-has-all-been-said silences between couples in a positive light. The song depicted these silences as peaceful ports in the storm of everyday life. I listened to the CD every day for a few weeks on my five-minute drive back and forth to the office, playing "Easy Silence" repeatedly, but I eventually became familiar with all of the first six songs. While the short drive to the office did not allow me enough time to become familiar with the second half of the CD, the Glenn storm did.

"The Voice Inside My Head," song ten on the CD, became the one that would sometime later transport me back to you, both on the stormy beach and during the peaceful aftermath. With the strumming of the first three chords, I simultaneously fell into a bottomless pit and lounged in a warm pool of sunshine. In your endless absence, I could see you and smell you and feel you. I felt both the pathos of the moment when the ferocious storm pinned your ears back and the serenity when we were all together safe in the car. You were gone forever, but I knew how to bring you back. I had heard the song before, but while sitting in the car that day, I discovered it.

I discovered it at a time when we had just strengthened the bond between us by our willing submission to the unbridled fury of the weather, a meteorological mood that we usually enjoyed from the dry side of a picture window, or protected in an interior room of the house. I still do not know exactly what the song is about, and I knew even less about it then. It seems that the songwriter is expressing her doubt about her current conventional life and wondering how life would have been different if she had made a different, riskier choice in the past. She questions her conventional good life at the same time she strives to believe in it. The lyrics are full of longing and nostalgia, just the type of song to take one back to a previous poignant moment. In my case, the first volley of chords strummed on an acoustic guitar brought you back at the price of an intense ache of longing for you.

When we returned home that day, the latent meteorologist in me had to see the radar of the storm we had experienced in the raw. As I suspected, we had been out in what the National Weather Service reckoned a severe thunderstorm. The radar loop showed that a bright yellow blob speckled with red passed over the beach while we were there. Just as with stoplights and street signs, red signals suggest more danger than yellow. I was disappointed that there had not been more red on the radar, because, from where I stood on the beach, yellow's caution hardly captured the peril we experienced.

****

During the excitement of our first trip to the beach north of Glenn, Cindy and I had not had enough time or suitable conditions to explore for stones and rocks. So we returned with you a couple of weeks later on a weekend morning. We stopped on the way in Glenn for brunch at the only restaurant in the town worthy of a trip while you rested in the car. The day was gray and cool for early September, the sort of day that invites few to the beach. We went for a long stroll on the beach without passing anyone until it was time to leave. For you, the surf was disappointingly rough, so after barely getting your feet wet you wandered the beach, roaming between Cindy and me. The rocks were not out and the sand was in. We could not see through the rough surf, so we did not have an extraordinary rock-hounding day.

Everything about our second trip to the beach north of Glenn was mediocre or drab until we had to ascend the flights of stairs to the picnic area above. The ascent at the outset aroused little concern, because of the ease with which you had accomplished it during our first visit. But this time, the climb nearly killed you. By the time we made it a third of the way up, you rested like you had just run a series of killer wind sprints. By the time we made it up the next third, you planted yourself on your belly like you planned to stay the night. We waited several minutes for you to recuperate and then gave you a coaxing tug on your leash; we entreated you with soothing voice-commands, but these literally fell on deaf ears. Finally, in fits and starts, you dragged yourself up half of the remaining distance and plopped down in a state of exhaustion that exceeded all previous states of exhaustion. Even after waiting for what seemed enough time for you to regenerate, an old man's catnap, you did not budge with a firm tug on the leash. You did not resist because you had no energy to resist. You had a dead battery, it seemed, and we had no tow service for canines. We could not just leave you there; carrying your fragile bones up the steps may have done more harm than good; we needed a gurney, but you would not have laid on it anyway.

At the moment we depleted our ideas, you mustered the energy to climb to the top with enough ease that I thought you had been holding out on us. But we knew you did not have a malingering bone in you. You sunk down into the ground at the top of the stairs and closed your eyes. Instead of panting with the exertion, you lay lifeless barely breathing. We had never seen anything like it; we thought that we had literally sucked the life right out of you.

Izzy, even though you slowed down with age, it was still

difficult to translate your aging into human terms. In human years, you were 80 or 90 depending on which scale we used, but you looked too robust to consider you a frail octogenarian. However, at that moment, I could only think of you in human terms, that we had driven you into a massive heart attack. What was I thinking making you climb ten flights of stairs when your tissues had aged to the equivalent of an eighty or ninety year old man? I would not have recommended in my wildest moments that any of my patients who had been ill for months climb the stairs to the tenth floor instead of taking the elevator. I had seen you exhausted, but this was more than profound exhaustion. This was last rights exhaustion. You still lay motionless with your snout between your paws and your eyelids closed. You had melted into the earth forever like the Wicked Witch of the West after she was doused with water.

You had two visitors from a multi-generational family picnicking in the park during your near-death experience. The first was a heavyset Hispanic woman, probably the grandmother, who seemed to understand just how tired you were. We told her about the trek that had brought about your motionless state. She somehow seemed to know that you were going to be all right and at a subliminal level communicated that to me. Your next visitor was a child from the same family, emboldened by his grandmother, who still had an innate fascination and fear of a big majestic dog, even when it appeared to be dead. He wanted to pet you. With our permission, his small hand reached for your head tentatively as if a magnet drew it forward while a puppet string restrained it; he patted your head a couple of times and watched you for another half minute before wandering off. Still you lay there motionless. While you received these visitors, I do not recall giving you as much attention as the little boy had given you. I was still too mortified.

You lay there motionless long enough for Cindy to mention backing the van through the park to the edge of the bluff so that we could lift you into the car. How or why you finally did lift your head and open your eyes, I do not know to this day. Did your heart recover enough to pump blood to your brain? Did a pain in your chest subside enough that you could focus on lifting your head? Did it take that long to finally feel your muscles again? Did an immense wave of nausea finally pass? Where had you been? My medical diagnostic abilities deserted me. We were able to entice you to your feet and you walked across the park like nothing happened. Had you been one of those injured pro football players who walks off the field after being surrounded by medical personnel for 10 minutes, you would have received an ovation from the entire stadium. As it was, you received the accolades of two tremendously relieved pet owners. Needless to say, we never returned to that stretch of Lake Michigan again during your lifetime.

One other frightening incident occurred on one of our beach excursions. It may seem that we took you to the beach against medical advice, but since it always sparked your interest in life, it was just as much just what the doctor ordered. Going to the beach therefore became our mission. Most excursions were unremarkable, and this other incident was merely a minor piece nestled in the middle of a typical peaceful, beautiful evening escape to the beach when our hometown temporarily became a vacation paradise. During the early period of your final six weeks, you showed some of your usual zest for retrieving boulders from the lake. However, as your exertions took a greater toll on your hips and your medications made you listless, you lost interest after retrieving a few substandard boulders from the lake floor and dropping them back in the surf before you reached the beach. Often the surf was just too rough on your hips. Almost certainly, if you were a human, you would have felt more comfortable with a cane some days and a walker on others. When your interest in retrieving boulders peaked, you usually hung close to me because I was the stone-thrower. When your interest began to wane, you wandered back and forth between Cindy and me, and sometimes you seemed disconnected in your own silent world.

This evening, you began with me, first chasing a couple stones and then walking in the surf to feel the boulders beneath your feet. As was our routine, I remained where stones piled in profusion near the mouth of Deerlick Creek and Cindy strolled south down the beach. While you usually took center stage in our lives at the time, on the beach, we immersed ourselves in the beach gems of a geologic convergence zone, where beautiful stones from the earth's foundry deposited by glaciation overlapped with fossils left behind by an ancient shallow sea. You sensed our obsession and began to wander on your own. I watched you meander south toward Cindy and dawdle around her, assuming that you had attached yourself to her and that you would follow her south. I also assumed that Cindy knew you were there and would keep her third eye on you.

Still, I did not completely relax my charge for you. I would study the stones in a given area within my reach, hone in on streaks of red and orange, swatches of blue and green, or striped patterns. When I exhausted one area, I would scoot to an adjacent arc and begin the process again. When my luck evaporated or my eye became super-saturated, I rested my eyes on the waves that stretched to the horizon, or on the beach that stretched south toward the plume of steam from the nuclear plant. You were not hanging as close to Cindy as usual and ambled to the dune grass at the edge of the beach at times. Your movement lacked purpose, either too tired or in too much pain to indulge your obsession. Though we had relaxed our focus on you, I relied upon your heightened attachment to us and your curbed desire to roam to keep you close by. So when I first looked up and did not see you anywhere, I figured that I just missed you in my initial cursory survey. Even after my second survey sharpened by squinted eyes, I was not yet alarmed. Only when I did not spot you after walking further south, scanning the water, scanning the dune grass, and then scanning the water again, approaching close enough to Cindy that she could hear my raised voice, did I become alarmed. Suddenly the gently rolling waves looked dark, hungry, and deadly.

"Have you seen Izzy?" I yelled to Cindy.

"No. I thought he was with you," she responded unconcerned.

"He wandered toward you fifteen minutes ago. Didn't you see him?" I had seen him within 10 or 15 feet of her, behind her, but he had no need to announce his presence. I was not accusing her. Your missing was not her problem; it was our problem.

"I didn't see him. I thought he was still with you." Then she said reassuringly, "I'm sure he's somewhere." She had not begun to reach my pitch of distress.

I understand now that you were in the process of giving up the water that you loved, but I did not understand this then. I could not imagine you wandering off in the woods when there was a body of water nearby. You must have swum toward the sunset as a fitting swansong before you realized that you were out too far. You were trying to make your way back to shore when you tired out and were pulled under. I looked for you bobbing among the trivial white caps. If I watched and waited long enough, the surf would surely deliver you back to me.

I was aware of discordant emotions—if you had

drowned, it would have been a natural death in your own time on your own terms, and it would have been over with; I would not have to face it again, and that somehow was a relief; but it grieved me to think that you may have suffered and died terrified without me. Besides I had not said my goodbyes nor was I ready to. No, the sense of relief did not outweigh the mounting grief. I had not yet reached the same level of hysteria as Cindy when she could not find you that day I impounded you in the back of the van, but I was getting a big dose of it. Like her, I believed that you had wandered off to die, but rather than going to your elephant graveyard on dry land, I imagined you succumbed in the disinterested lethal embrace of one of the loves of your life.

Cindy, who never did completely leave the peaceful pastime of discovering beach gems for my irrational place, was right about you. You were somewhere—somewhere on dry land. Sandy paths cut through the upward slope of dune grass along the eastern edge of the beach to parcels of land that would one day become home sites. You had wandered up the first or second one I came to. You were in a shaded clearing chewing on grass, whiling away your evening. If I had not known better, your oblivious air suggested a passive-aggressive act. But I was too relieved to hold on to any ill feelings. You may have lost the energy to spread the contagious joy of retrieving boulders, but I would accept a couple more years of dry land behavior any day. Eventually, your amblings through the dune grass—a canine lion lumbering in the Savannah grass at sunset—became one of my fondest and most peaceful images. I was learning that I had the ability to adapt to your losses, that I could do it as long as you roamed our world.

****

As long as you could stumble on all four legs, you never did completely lose your instinct to enter the water with the right incentive. One very busy day at work when I had the extra responsibility of covering the South Haven Hospital newborn unit, I recognized that a beautiful sunset escorted by caressing breezes was in the offing. For days, perhaps weeks, my internal engine had clicked into overdrive so that I might use every remaining opportunity to take you to the beach; some part of me must have known that these opportunities were nearing their end. I squared away enough at work to create a window in my evening to rush home and then to the beach with my family, you and Cindy. Watching those that I loved indulge their passions, Cindy with her newfound photography and you in the company of water, would provide the perfect break before finishing my work on the newborn unit in the hospital.

In spite of my best efforts, by the time I arrived home, the sun had already slipped below the horizon. I had expected that Cindy would understand my tardiness and remain enthusiastic about our beach visit that evening. Earlier that summer, we had learned while watching sunsets from Evergreen Bluff that the best part of the sunset arrived after the sun sank below the horizon. It was a little-known secret that Dave Witte, a retired physician and photographer, shared with us while we watched the kaleidoscope of colors from pre-sunset to darkness from the bluff in front of his house. Dave, who had seen many seasons of lakeside sunsets, had become a connoisseur of sunsets and had made a science of rating the beauty of these transitional spectacles on a scale of one to ten. The evening he imparted his lesson he rated the sunset a fifteen. Still, a few months later, I had to convince Cindy that we had missed only a fraction of the sunset and most of it was still to come. She was eventually persuaded, but not without briefly making me feel unappreciated for my efforts. In time, her frost would thaw enough to completely immerse herself in the evolution of the horizon.

The deep, sugar-sand beach south of the pier and lighthouse at the mouth of the Black River offered both an unobstructed view of the sunset and a slightly obstructed view of the sunset, the latter with a quaint lighthouse in the foreground. By that late September evening, summer tourism had ended and only a couple handfuls of the locals remained after the wholesale departure when the last red sliver of sun disappeared. Those who sought the solitude of dusk welcomed the belief that the sun's disappearance marked the sunset's single magical moment; Dr. Witte's insight was a secret well-kept. Cindy took her camera and tripod and became one of the few anonymous solitary figures on the wide beach in the deepening dusk. She opened her shutter toward the glow on the horizon.

You and I strolled together on the beach. As I expected, you initially made a slow beeline toward the water. The beach's sugary sand and stone-free surf were easy on bare feet, but had little to offer your obsession. I looked for anything to throw, a waterlogged root or a rotting branch. The surf was barely rippled and would have been easy on your aching hips. None of it mattered; it did not spark your interest. I tagged along as you walked aimlessly on the gentle slope of the beach. You were as interested in the dune grass far from the water as the shoreline and you moved between the two as slowly as the moon climbed the eastern horizon.

We wandered back toward the beach where Cindy was setting up for her final and most striking shots of the horizon. Night reigned over the sky, except for the western horizon, transforming Cindy, you, and me into featureless figures in motion. You sensed that you were now with both of us. Close by, the water shimmered darkly. By now, you had been wandering for fifteen or twenty minutes with a couple brief rests in the sand, and you seemed about ready to go home.

Under these circumstances, the near-night of the day and the near-night of all your senses, how you saw or heard that group of ducks, I do not know. But there always had been activities that you would do only when both Cindy and I were present. A rawhide bone would lay in the living room for days hardly disturbed, even when slathered with peanut butter, until an evening when both Cindy and I were present together; then you would suddenly find it and eat most of it in an hour. When you heard those ducks with both Cindy and I in the vicinity, something in you ignited. You did not dash into the water, but for the first time that evening, you ambled with purpose into the quiet surf and disappeared into the ebbing twilight in the direction of the ducks. I thought that you were taking your last swim, not because you were going to die in the next week, but because you were not going to make it back from this one. I had my day clothes on and did not relish the idea of going in after you in the autumn-cool water. On the other hand, how fitting it would be if this were your last swim, literally swimming into the sunset.

You never did catch a duck or a goose on the water. When you were at your best, they taunted you by letting you swim within 10 feet and then they doubled the distance, flapping the water with their low trajectory flight. But this time, you gave up long before achieving that kind of proximity and returned to shore safely. I remarked, "You're still one crazy dog!" You were too feeble to acknowledge your return to dry land by shimmying the water from your fur.

Cindy finished her series of shots near the pier and we started back toward the van. Before reaching the van, another view caught Cindy's fancy and she separated from us again. You wandered aimlessly with me in tow, but eventually I used the leash to lead you back to the van in the parking lot fifty yards from the shoreline. By then, Cindy had completed her sunset shots but was nowhere in sight. I suspected that the skate park at the northern end of the parking lot had attracted her, but I had no way of confirming it without making the long walk with you.

For me, the mild caressing breezes and the brilliant moonlit sky had lost their charm. The window of time I had opened to enjoy this evening had long since closed and I was beginning to feel oppressed by the work I had left to do that evening. I could see that you had spent yourself and wanted to put you in the back of the van. By then, you no longer had the strength to climb in the car without a ramp. For this purpose, we had been using a carpet-covered piece of plywood that required two people for its use, one to hold the ramp steady at the base while the other pulled you up the ramp with your leash.

My frustration took risks that patience would have averted. I knew that the ramp might collapse if I set it up on a steep incline in the parking lot. To reduce the incline, I wanted to back the van up to the deep curb that ran along the beach, but I had no one to watch you while I turned the van around and backed it up to the curb. To you, I used a few choice words in reference to Cindy while I considered my options, which would have been unnecessary if Cindy was where she was supposed to be. Your illness had opened up the doors to a beautiful harmony that I felt helpless to sustain in that moment. Not only was my anger not going to bring her back more quickly, it was going to interpose a few discordant chords in the Izzy symphony, the composition of the final phase of your life.

You were the first to pay the price for my rashness. I decided to set the ramp up in the parking lot anyway at the steep angle required. To minimize this angle, I had to minimize the amount of the board overlapping the back of the van. Then I pulled you up the bowing ramp until your front legs were in the van and your hind legs were on the carpeted ramp. At that moment, the ramp slipped off the lip of the van and crashed to the parking lot, leaving you hanging half in and half out, with your front legs stretched painfully in the back of the van and your back paws on the ground. I was horrified. Your master to whom you had entrusted your safe ascension into the car, who was supposed to make life easier for you, may have just ruined your painful swollen elbow for good. Your front legs would not support getting you into the van so I encircled your chest and helped you out of the van. What happened to our beautiful evening? I had destroyed it. Why had I made what I felt was a minor heroic effort to be there for this outcome? I directed my wrath inward and toward the skate park across the parking lot. I bristled with regret for ruining such a large proportion of the rest of your life and with remorse for my own inability to get a grip on the ugly side of my nature.

You seemed to survive my anger more unscathed than your human companions. When Cindy returned, I was able to pull you up the secured ramp as if no previous mishap had occurred. My anger caught her by surprise and sent her spiraling from the lofty place the beautiful evening had taken her. Helplessly, I donned the black hat and caused my damsel some distress. No malice from her had been intended, yet I could not stop myself from heaping it on her. A thousand times I would recompose that part of our symphony if I could.

Only later would Cindy rescue the evening for me with an electronic memory inside her camera. With a long exposure, she had caught the orange-red of the sunset's cloud-shredded afterglow. Angling into the lake from the right dividing the picture horizontally, sky from water, was the pier with its series of arches supporting the catwalk that led to the lighthouse. With each sentinel-like arch was a glowing torch that sent a rippled ribbon of fire onto the surf. In one of her pictures, you were there, barely visible, in pursuit of ducks.

****

The evening we took you to the beach for the final time was a sweater-weather overcast Monday, ideal for those who seek solitude and a calm surf. Neither Cindy nor I knew that it would be your last time at the beach. Only your eternal earthly departure would give us that perspective and anoint this evening with special significance. At the time, while we prepared, putting Cindy's camera, tripod and lenses, and the buckets for stones in the car, you expressed some of your usual zeal for a van ride to the beach. From your daylong inertia on the living room carpet, you moved yourself in the middle of things in the mudroom, announcing your desire to go wherever we were going. Moments later you pranced up the ramp into the car.

At the beach, you no longer charged the wavy surf, but you still enjoyed dawdling in the shallow rocky mouth of the Deerlick Creek where it entered Lake Michigan. I threw a few stones into the rock-lined creek that carved a new path every few days near the lake. It was no more than ankle-deep near the lake so that diving for the rocks was not an option. You pawed at the rocks and mouthed a few of them, but you did not retrieve any. I was quietly disappointed in how quickly you lost interest. Your waning interest, a sure indication of how bad you felt, drained my own in finding stony treasures, but I accepted it and mourned it as another incremental step toward what was still a surprisingly vague sense of your eternal absence.

Before you simply lay down on the beach, you wandered aimlessly, not ready to lie down, but without energy or will to tackle the shallow current. I was initially too engrossed in my hunt to notice the moment you lay down. When I did finally notice you, it was with surprise and pathos. You were sitting there alone in your silent world, perhaps spending one of your last hours, while Cindy stalked the beach trying out a new telephoto lens and I lost myself in igneous trinkets. I decided to sit beside you to keep you company. After all, I had come to the beach to put the life back in you, perhaps because it put life back in me. I could not enjoy myself on that cool overcast evening if I sensed that you could not. If you were done, I was ready to go, but Cindy had not yet finished her mission. As I moved to take my seat behind you, I saw her moving north in the dune grass behind us, setting up for another series of pictures.

There was a little consolation knowing that Cindy was getting practice using her new telephoto lens. The sense that I was just killing time until it was time to go was gnawing away at my mission for that moment, to make this time with you meaningful. I felt hollow and inept as I pet your head, hoping you might thrust it back gleefully or at least acknowledge its presence. Time played its ambiguous game, each second painfully long while all I really wanted was more time with you. The drab horizon insinuated itself into the features of the surf and further beclouded the beauty of these moments with you. I had surrendered to the sorrow of the moment, for you, but more probably for myself. I was just waiting for Cindy to finish so that I could escape my disappointment.

Once again, Cindy's eye memorialized the best part of this evening, converting my memory of it from a series of disappointing moments to one that more than any other expressed the relationship between you and me. While she was behind us in the dune grass, I had no idea that we were her subjects. She saw something from behind that I could not see looking ahead. She did not show me her shots until after you were gone, waiting for a time when I had sufficiently recovered to bear them. Yet she recognized their power to heal and did not want to wait too long. In the black and white photo, she had captured the essence of the relationship, the element that caused me to sit beside you in the first place. And she had cleansed the moment of the self-pity that had invaded me at the time. The essence of the pictures was that I was sitting beside you because the totality of your life had engendered a deep human bond that could only be described as love, not affection only, not loyalty only, not commitment only, but love.

Cindy liked the photo most in which both of us were looking out at the horizon. You and I were large in the foreground joined by my outstretched arm that petted the scruff of your neck. A thick stripe of gray sky and the rippled lake, softened by the long exposure, occupied three-fourths of the picture and provided a background that was consonant with the mood of its subjects. You and I seemed united in reverie, contemplating the lake that stretched to the western horizon. The picture truly deserved to be entitled with the hackneyed expression, "Man's Best Friend," because it captured in a generic way the human-canine umbilical cord. In another picture in the series, your head arched backwards in response to my petting hand. I am looking at you with an uplifted heart. At first, I liked that picture more, but I am moved by the poignancy of both of them together, one affirming life and the other foretelling the hereafter.

Many patients have commented on the black and white photos now hanging in my examining rooms, not only because they are aesthetically pleasing photos, but also because they see the same sentiment in them that I do. They wonder if I am in the photo. I respond somewhat sheepishly, "Yes, I am in the picture, but it is a picture of my dog." I respond this way, not only because I am embarrassed to have photos of myself hanging in my rooms, even if viewed from the rear, but because I am not the subject—either you are or we are. Now that I have changed the subject to you, I tell them, "That is four days before he was gone forever." You see, in my mind, you looked so handsome, so robust, like such a wonderful companion, even four days before you died. Your presence in the picture with me so close to your death communicated the depth and freshness of your absence. That picture meant so much more to me because it was taken so close to the most singular moment in your life. How hollow the moment seemed at the time; how poignant it became when viewed across the chasm of your death.

I had no idea on the day these pictures were taken that I would be helping you four days later cross the threshold. A life transpires like the sun as it crosses the sky from sunrise to sunset. It appears to race at the beginning of the day and at the end of the day. At its peak, around midday, it hardly seems to move at all. Some lives last as long as a midwinter day; others the length of a midsummer day. For lives that end suddenly and prematurely at midday, it seems they were snuffed by an eclipse, or that they fell from the sky like Icarus. In your case, I knew that the sun of your life was low in the western sky, but I had no idea that on the day memorialized in Cindy's pictures that such a tiny sliver of it was sitting on the horizon. At the time, I functioned best looking forward in innocence, believing that your sun was setting slowly, the entire sphere still above the horizon in the western sky. But in retrospect, I cannot help being struck most profoundly by those moments when the western horizon was eclipsing the final crescent of your sun.

*

****

The reality that you were going to die was never an issue between Cindy and me, though we rarely discussed it. About when you were going to die, on the other hand, Cindy and I had contrasting, but balancing outlooks. Cindy's optimistic, innocent perspective was a balm for my relatively realistic, informed perspective. Cindy had accepted the possibility that we might need to catheterize you for the next two years of your life. We had become, it seemed, such experts that we could take the procedure on the road anywhere in the country.

She researched several road trips in which you were included, to Nova Scotia and then to the Canadian Rockies in Banff or Jasper National Parks. We planned road trips only, delaying any travel that required air travel, because we did not want to leave you.

I enjoyed listening to these far-fetched plans, because Cindy was expressing to me that you meant as much to her as you did to me. Cindy loved travel and most of the destinations at the top of her list would have required a flight, but she was willing to put those plans on hold indefinitely for you. Standing in front of our large mirror preparing for the day or relaxing on the love seat in front of the fireplace winding down from it, I expressed my approval for these road trips and even some muted excitement about the prospect of traveling with you. She made me believe that we had our own Travels With Charley in the future with you that extended months or years beyond what my unspoken medical experience and innate doubt imagined. I did not express my doubts, because I needed her innocent dreams even more than she did. If I had expressed my doubts, not only would her sustaining dreams have dried up, but she also would have begun to see you through my eyes and brought my simmering worries about you to a boil. I wanted to adopt her view that what I perceived as the exhaustion of age and illness was really peacefulness and resignation.

Inevitably, a time did come when I could no longer maintain my silence about your future. But, I first had to let go of a burden that I had unknowingly accepted. I was overwhelming myself with not only keeping you alive, but also with keeping a dimming past alive—thus running you to the beach, taking you for car rides, feeding you wherever you lay, regulating the amount of your urine, willing you to eat, willing you to smile, willing a nugget of canine joy so that I might savor it. I was not just emptying your bladder. Many times when addressing the families of a dying loved one, I would tell them that even if we offered their loved one everything modern medicine had to offer, their loved one had to provide the rest. By this I meant that even modern medicine cannot save someone in whom too many systems are failing. Yet I had taken the responsibility of doing it all for you, against my own medical advice. My own pain from watching you suffer one loss after another forced me to take this final major step toward letting you go.

After this realization one morning in the shower, I interrupted Cindy's lyrical discourse in front of the mirror about plans for a trip with you to Banff the following summer 10 months away. "10 months" away seemed an inconceivable miracle. "I don't know if he's even going to make it through the week," I sobbed. For Cindy, it was a cloudburst from sunny skies. Not only was she surprised by my grief, she was arrested by what she understood to be my medical opinion.

"Why didn't you tell me? I didn't know you were thinking that." It had taken me that long to recognize that I had to prepare her too.

We buried you four days later.

****

There were times when Cindy had good reason to be optimistic. I shared it. There were periods of smooth sailing—during the early stages of your decline, we became so proficient at catheterizing you that it took no time at all, and subsequently when your bladder function improved, we hardly needed to catheterize you, maybe once every two or three days. If you did require catheterization when your stream dwindled, we took it for granted that the catheter would slide right into the bladder as long as necessary. I believed that things would go as smoothly for you as it did for a teenage boy in my practice who catheterized himself for over a decade after a case of encephalitis disrupted his bladder function. From start to finish, we were getting our job done with you in five minutes, a minor inconvenience. Once, you resisted the catheter enough that I was unable to get it in, but I had no trouble threading it the next fifteen times. I realized that one time I failed how much you must have trusted us to handle your penis, because you had powerful muscles available to you to retract it into its prepuce and make my job a living hell. But this one time was the exception. Mostly it was automatic, from the moment you laid yourself down virtually unassisted on your left side to my record keeping at the end.

A tidal wave upended our smooth sailing one evening ten days before the end. It overtook us unexpectedly when your well-being seemed to be gaining momentum. I recorded on your urine diary that you were still urinating regularly, feeling better overall, and seemed to be in less pain. However, I still judged that your weakened urine stream suggested that your bladder was filling to a point of inefficiency. I had last catheterized you without difficulty two days earlier. You lay down with a little more hesitation than usual because you had two days to forget our routine, but you were still extremely cooperative compared to your more youthful rebelliousness. After we set you up, I pushed the catheter toward your rear and though it seemed to disappear in your prepuce, it was not clearly sliding up the shaft of your penis. I tried the usual maneuvers but you resisted me so much with the muscles that control your penis that I finally had to take a break. You were snorting and throwing your muzzled snout and shoulders in my direction as if I was violating you this time. Cindy redirected her attention from connecting the syringe to the catheter to calming you down. When my hand had rested enough and you calmed down, I repeated the process and hit the same obstruction. When I pulled the catheter out, for the first time there was bloody mucous on the end of the catheter. When I imagined what I had done to you, I came unhinged in a way that I had never done with a human procedure. I had thrown a stick of dynamite in your lifeline. The obstruction was not the natural result of 60 plus catheterizations in a dog; rather, it was my sloppy technique that had set the stage for your demise.

    I recovered my composure enough to make one more attempt with a brand new catheter with the same outcome. Frazzled, I whipped off your muzzle and ran to the kitchen to get you a biscuit, your well-earned reward for the torture you had just endured. Cindy was less alarmed than I was and remained optimistic about our attempt the next morning, because she lacked the experience to visualize the damaged tissues inside the bone of your penis. I was already dreading my attempt the next morning. Later that evening, to my relief, you produced a thin urinary stream, fizzling my dynamite scenario. You could get liquid out; I just could not get a solid in.

    The following morning I set up like usual, pulling a catheter from the bin of dilute Betadine, wiping it off with an alcohol pad, taking it by the funneled end to the living room, and then lying its bowed length on a couple of fresh paper towels. I was more prepared to fail than to succeed. Whether a self fulfilling prophecy or the result of residual swelling from my botched attempt the evening before, my catheter only managed to retrieve blood and mucous from your urinary tract. My desperation reached new heights, because you had not even dribbled earlier that morning. If I could not catheterize you, you could not empty you bladder, and if you could not empty your bladder, you would reach the same level of misery that you did the morning we took you to the Emergency room, and that would be the end of you.

Again, your crisis took place in the middle of a workweek on a day that I had a full slate of patients. When I arrived at the office, I did not try to modify the perception that I was rearranging my life for a crisis with my dog. I examined my schedule and immediately entreated the staff to cancel a window of patients in the afternoon so that I could take you to the veterinarian. My staff did one better and canceled most of my afternoon, leaving only the first two or three afternoon patients. They responded more to my level of distraction than the source of it. Though most of my office staff always showed a great deal of interest and sympathy in our plight, I never felt comfortable revealing how much you affected me. I believed that there was something wrong with me, that there was something unnatural and pathetic about my attachment to you. My father had died nine months earlier and they had not seen me this overwrought during his final weeks.

Though compelled to write my love story, I am still bothered that others might believe it is self-indulgent and excessive. Wouldn't my time and energy be better spent solving the health crisis? Am I merely exposing my pathology rather than sharing a story that will resonate with the rest of the dog-loving world? Perhaps it is the pathology that we find most interesting in the first place. Am I becoming one of the people who feels worse when a dog dies in the movie than when one of the main human characters dies? Am I as obsessed as Jerry Shepherd, the main character in the movie Eight Below, who traveled across United States, devoting considerable resources and risking human lives, just to find out if his dogs were alive? On the other hand, one would not have stranded a team of humans in the worst conditions of the Antarctic. The human team made the choice in the first place to leave the dogs rather than any humans.

Your veterinarian was not scheduled in the office that day. First I tried her at home and talked to her husband who told me that she would be back within the hour. When I did not hear from her, I tried calling her office to see if her staff might know where she was. Her reception personnel never erected false roadblocks that prevented me from talking to their boss. If she was available, they would not say, "She's with a client now". They would say, "Just one minute; we'll find her for you." I also never felt that they considered me demanding or a nuisance; they achieved the proper tone of empathy. Perhaps their leader had communicated to them that she had a special interest in your case because it was so unusual, or maybe they treated everyone like a VIP. In any case, she came right to the phone. Once again, she agreed to accommodate my schedule as long as I could bring you in before she went on a field trip with one of her three children.

Once again, she was ready for you when we arrived that afternoon about an hour before the field trip. While I waited very briefly for her, I remember thinking how robust you seemed in spite of the emergency that precipitated your visit. It had to be evident to everyone that if it were not for the simple problem with your bladder, you had a great deal of life left in you. Who could think of putting down such a fine animal? She greeted us in the waiting room as was her routine, and rather than taking you back to the large procedure room, she took us to a small examining room. She had set out several catheters of varying calibers to thread into your bladder. One catheter was less than half the diameter of the one I had failed to pass into your bladder earlier that day. Rather than dismissing my efforts by attempting to pass the large catheter, she prepared the smaller catheter.

We decided to catheterize you sitting on the floor of the small exam room. I took Cindy's role of giving you comforting strokes and holding your hind leg out of the way.

From this vantage point, I had an opportunity to examine her technique and compare it to mine. If your penis were the head of a turtle, she managed to coax it out as if it was stretching for a juicy berry whereas I coaxed it out just far enough to check for a potential predator like a raccoon. When she threaded the catheter, she kept it out as if it were feasting in complete safety, whereas for me, it ducked back in as if it were avoiding the swat of a big fat paw. When I mentioned the difference later, she responded, "I've been doing it for years." Having done it sixty times, I did not feel like a beginner. I would discover in a few days that my two-glove technique was much of the problem. When I did the procedure without the gloves, I instantly became more dexterous and "experienced."

My heart leaped when she passed the small catheter without difficulty into your bladder. It may have taken five to ten times as long to withdraw one-third the volume of urine, but she had given you another lease on life! After struggling to fill the smaller syringe four or five times, your veterinarian decided to try the usual larger catheter. She passed it with minimal resistance and we drained three-fourths quart of urine from your bladder in five minutes using the coordinated technique that Cindy and I had developed at home. I was so encouraged by our success that I believed my failures of the previous morning and evening were merely temporary snags. Nevertheless, before my departure, your vet prepared a doggy bag for me that included several catheters of varying diameters. She wanted to give me options so that I would not ignite the blaze of desperation she had just extinguished. I thought that she was being slightly overcautious, but her decision would soon prove to be prescient.

Cindy and I had our next opportunity to catheterize you the following morning. It did not go as well as I had hoped, but this time I kept my wits about me. When the usual large gauge catheter did not pass, I was able to pass a smaller catheter fairly easily into your bladder. Then, I retried the normal catheter, more than twice the diameter, and it passed through with a small amount of resistance. I had achieved the desired outcome by remaining patient, using the model your veterinarian had given the day before, and drawing upon my medical experience, but a problem was still there. The necessity of resorting to extra measures left me with some trepidation when it came to the next catheterization.

You also suffered a setback in the strength of your urinary stream. I was back to counting past 10 before your trickle began, and the thrill of watching your golden stream vanished. Since you emptied smaller amounts each time we took you out to urinate, we had to take you out more often to keep your bladder at its most functional volume. This regimen taxed your arthritic hips and weary bones. When I gently tugged on your leash and sung my encouraging words, you began to protest by remaining dead weight with a profound look of indifference.

The second catheterization after I took you to the veterinarian seemed to confirm that you had developed a partial blockage. For the first time, we completely drained your bladder with the smallest catheter available that slid, to my relief, into your bladder with minimal resistance. The amount of urine that previously would have required a couple minutes and a little over five easy draws with the large syringe took a half hour and seventeen relatively difficult draws with the smaller syringe.

The procedure suddenly had become much more onerous. Cindy suffered because she usually sat on the sofa behind you and had to lean over to do her job of detaching the catheter and holding it while I replaced the syringe. I believe she could have withstood the blood rushing to her head for a half hour if it had not been for the fecal smell that your urine developed in the final period. If it had not been an odor that came from you, my sensitive nose would not have withstood it either. By the end of the catheterization process, Cindy had a headache and had to excuse herself because she thought she might vomit.

The palm of my right hand and my wrist absorbed most of the abuse from pulling back on the plunger. The foot of the plunger drove into the palm of my right hand each time I pulled back on it by vigorously cocking my wrist toward my thumb. By the end of the catheterization process, I felt a sharp pain in my wrist each time I pulled the plunger back. Later in the day, I noticed the palm of my hand was black and blue and puffy. Lifting weights every other day and occasionally wielding a scalpel at the office apparently had not conditioned me for the repetitive mechanics of emptying your bladder.

Given the extra time required and the wear and tear on the living instruments of my livelihood, my hands and wrist, the next morning, I tried the larger catheter one last time. I encountered the same resistance. From then on, we committed ourselves to using the tiny catheter. Cindy especially accepted the setback in stride and could foresee taking the extra time to catheterize you while we explored the Canadian Rockies. We did make some adjustments so that the procedure was not as onerous. In the evening, we did it during a television show that we might have watched anyway (though the TV was to my back, so I usually listened to it; in the morning CNN Headline News serenaded us.

The length of the process may have tested your patience at first, but with time, you were spending most of your life on one of your sides anyway. Once the catheter was in, you usually relaxed for as long as it took, even when we mercifully stopped putting the muzzle on you. Sometime around the time we decided to do without the muzzle, I stopped wearing gloves for the catheterizations. The muzzle, we stopped, both because it was the most degrading part of the process for you (we had always used it as an instrument of discipline, or punishment) and because you were becoming too weak to protest. The gloves, I had worn, up to that point, to protect your bladder from the bacteria on my hands. However, when it became clear that, in spite of our best efforts, your urine had become infected with a bacterium producing foul-smelling byproducts that was not responding to a potent antibiotic, I threw caution to the wind and, in so doing, threw the greatest hassle of the entire procedure out the window. Once I catheterized you without gloves, something Cindy had recommended weeks earlier, my only regret was that I had not listened to her when she first brought it up; maybe things would have gone differently. But who could have foreseen then that the odor of your urine would fill up a 20 by 20 foot room with 12-foot ceilings?

****

On a Saturday, within two days of initiating our use the narrow catheter, we were rewarded for our efforts, though at first it seemed that your stream had suffered a permanent setback. That morning, before we catheterized you, you lifted your leg to urinate without emptying a drop. Then, lowering your bladder to the ground, you pushed with all your might before walking forward several feet to try again, each time without results. To steady myself, I tried to follow a principle from my medical practice when things got difficult and I struggled to stay afloat emotionally. When discouraged by the patient's slow response, the complexity of the problems, or the patient's resistance, I formulated an objective plan based upon best assessment of the situation and an appropriate standard of care, and stuck with it. Though doubt persisted, any other plan would have only been more likely to lead to failure. More often than not, the optimal plan required the most work and monitoring, but one just never knew the outcome. In your case, our plan was to keep your urine volumes low and give you plenty of opportunities to urinate on your own. This meant being with you whenever possible. In part to accomplish our therapeutic goals, but mainly to be with you whenever possible, we took you on our planned trip to Kalamazoo.

Cindy had bought tickets months earlier when your health was not in doubt to see Elton John's Aida. You were excited to be going with us somewhere in the car. Before we left, I let you urinate expecting disappointment, but to my surprise, you emitted a decent stream nonchalantly as if you had been holding out on us. We arrived early at the Miller Auditorium on the campus of Western Michigan University in Kalamazoo with just enough time to find a place to park in the shade of an outbuilding surrounded by pine trees and then take you for a walk. You gave a repeat performance with your urine stream. I went into the theater with a lighter heart and a less clouded, more receptive mind.

Though I had my doubts about a modern day Aida and would have much-preferred Verdi's original in Italian, I was moved by Elton John's adaptation. It is a Romeo and Juliet type story set in the Middle East. Aida, a Nubian princess, is captured and enslaved by the heir to the Egyptian throne who subsequently falls in love with her. Aida and the prince are young, idealistic people whose love for each other makes them more tolerant without performing the same magic on those around them. Their love that could not exist on earth finds a sanctuary for all eternity when they are sent to a common tomb to die. Though the story and performances fanned my youthful flames, what I remember most about that day is your performance during intermission and your encore after the show. For my entertainment only, during intermission, while we walked together in warmed pine needles and sniffed their woodsy scent, you sent your golden ribbon earthward, not once but again and again. I reported your performance with delight to Cindy. After the play, while we walked around the grassy knoll that surrounded the outbuilding, waiting for the parking lot to empty, you gave several encores for both of us.

We finished the day with pizza that came highly recommended by one of my patients, who spoke enthusiastically about food in general and girded his large frame with years of connoisseurship. Though we found that fine pizza with organic, homemade ingredients takes four to five times as long to make as regular pizza, we were not disappointed. Pizza was transformed from fast food to a fine dining experience. Cindy and I made the most of our wait, enjoying the contemporary expressionistic paintings on the wall that transformed nature scenes into boldly colored fantasies. I wanted to take one home, but Cindy's practicality recognized that even in our house with 12-foot walls, we did not have one that would fit these large scenes. Our soft-spoken, diffident waiter struck me as a layover from the sixties, reminding me of a couple bearded schoolmates from my high school days, one who went on to be a talented musician and the other an astrophysicist. I wondered why he was wiling away his talents waiting tables in a restaurant known for its pizza. Overall, the place was folksy and classy like a Bob Dylan or Joan Baez song and transported Cindy and me most of the way back to our college days where we dined in the funkier restaurants in Durham and Chapel Hill, North Carolina.

We savored our pizza garnished with fresh tomato, onion, and garlic spread on a foundation of ideally proportioned tomato sauce and chef designed Italian cheeses, but we tucked away our crust for you. There was never too much crust on a pizza, only too little, because your share of every pizza meal was my crust, and Cindy's, in your last golden year. The tradition dated back to the touchdown tandem of Steve Young and Jerry Rice of the San Francisco 49ers when, on Sunday Nights, the entire family watched Sports Center while eating pizza from Pizza Hut. Waiting for my crust, you sat at my feet or stood with your head in my lap, usually soaking my pants with drool. Sometimes, I was finishing my last bite when you grabbed for your piece of crust. In the car on the way home, you mounted enough enthusiasm for the crust to give me another lift. Had the ramp not collapsed while getting you back in the van at the theatre, that afternoon and evening would have been perfectly joyous.

****

The following day, Sunday, we opened up more of our side yard to the heavens, for sunlight during the day and for stargazing at night. When you joined our human family as a six-week-old puppy five months after we moved into our new home, the idea of leaving as many trees as possible to preserve the sense that we were living in the woods rather than merely surrounded by them still appealed to us. However, over the almost-thirteen years of your life, the trees at the margin of the clearing had followed their heliocentric instincts into the clearing. Cindy, as her claustrophobia increased, cast a hostile eye on these marginal trees, some of which I had grown quite fond. She began to crave the sun as if she were a green plant, and, with her own need for sun came an urge to create a wilderness garden that required much more sun than was available in our yard. Her drive to create and change eventually hooked me. Already, I had expanded my range in felling trees when I cut down a 14-inch oak tree that was shielding a small ornamental cherry tree that I planted in honor of our 26th year of marriage. But mostly, I had taken my chainsaw guilt-free to sassafras trees that were weedy and straggly, no matter how large they grew. Sunday, you witnessed another segment of the most significant change we made to our land since you had become part of our family.

That Sunday, slightly warmer than the day before, was one of those days that begs for an outdoor project—pellucid early October skies, bug-free, and somewhere between short-sleeve or cotton long-sleeve temperatures. You remained with us in the work zone, occasionally doddering to a new spot to plant yourself. Inside, you would have crashed, but outdoors you remained attentive to our activity. Though I always made sure that you were not in the arc of the potential landing zone of a falling sassafras, you seemed to have a sixth sense that kept you out of harm's way. Mostly, you paid attention to Cindy's more peaceful activity. While I felled trees and cut them into manageable pieces, she pursued less destructive, quieter activities (though even with my chainsaw, your world was quiet). You doddered nearby, at first, while she piled branches for a later bonfire and dragged others off into the woods. You wandered back to the house with her while she prepared a mini-picnic of berry smoothies and Triscuits with humus and Jarlsburg Swiss cheese. Later as you lay in the grass open-mouthed in a gentle pant, you posed for candid pictures. Cindy viewed these pictures as the distillation of peacefulness. I recall sitting with the dog in these pictures briefly between intense periods of activity. I love these pictures that focused on your face, but instead of seeing a peaceful dog now, I see what my daily existence with you hid from me then—the profound weariness of advanced years.

You would not live to see the next addition to our yard—the dogwood that we planted on top of you. That Sunday was the day before I took you to Deerlick beach and sat with you while Cindy took pictures from the dune grass behind us. That Sunday was three days before I burst Cindy's bubble while standing in front of our large bathroom mirror, still wet from crying in the shower, and dashed her plans for our Travels With Izzy. That Sunday was three or four days before I started gathering information about how I needed to bury you. However, on that Sunday, I had no idea that it would be the last Sunday you would ever see.

****

I still thought that you were a very mature dog with a problem concentrating his urine and emptying his bladder, neither of which were fatal. I did suspect, however, that one or several of your medicines was taking a toll on you. I was giving you five medications, four of them wrapped up in cheese or roast beef, and the other, injected into the scruff of your neck or into your back between your hips. One made your bladder contract. Another relaxed the muscles that formed a sling beneath your bladder. Another was supposed to treat the bacteria that caused the foul odor of your urine. Another was supposed to lubricate your aching joints. The only one that I was sure was doing something required injections. It did significantly reduce your urine volume by making your kidneys concentrate it. It was this last medication, however, about which I had the greatest concern. I thought that it was slowly sapping your strength.

As it was not clear that any of the pills were helping you, I would periodically stop them. The antibiotic which was not eliminating the foul odor of your urine had the potential to make your joints and tendons ache. When you resisted getting up to urinate, I tried stopping it for a couple days without improvement. Still concerned that bacteria from your urine could enter your bloodstream and profoundly weaken you, I decided to give it to you once daily instead of twice daily. The medication that relaxed the muscles at the floor of your bladder had the potential to make you lightheaded; I had the least confidence that this medication made a difference. I would stop it for several days at a time, and then, when you had a bad day urinating, would restart it. During the last two weeks, I gave it to you very irregularly. The medication that made your bladder contract also had the potential to make you weak. I was never convinced that it helped, because you did not start urinating until I introduced the DDAVP that reduced your urine volumes. Still it made sense to give you a medication that made your bladder muscle contract, so I gave it to you most days until it became a major effort for you to get up. I did not want the medication to create the urge to urinate when you could not get up to relieve yourself.

The DDAVP was the miracle medication that made us believe, at first, that there was a light at the end of the tunnel of your urine problem. During a period that began shortly after starting the medication and ended with the fiasco inserting the larger catheter, you urinated on demand and with gusto. What's more, it made our job easier by reducing the volume we had to drain from your bladder. This action especially became important when we had to drain your bladder using the smaller catheter because doubling the volume would double a time already excessively long. I was vaguely aware that the medication could affect the salts in your blood like sodium and potassium, your fluid balance, and your kidney function. But theoretically (as we really had only weak evidence that your body wasn't making enough DDAVP, or desmopressin), your body needed it because your body was not making enough of it, just like a diabetic needs insulin. When I gave you the medication, you drank much less water and produced much less urine. You had been guzzling water so long that I became concerned while you were on the medication that you were not drinking enough.

I had discussed my concerns about the medication with your veterinarian a couple of weeks earlier, because I thought that it was causing malaise. She recommended reducing the frequency of dosing to once daily. At a time when you were urinating on demand, I tried this reduction only once. The next morning, you could not urinate at all and I had to drain a quart of urine from your bladder, five to ten times more than the previous catheterizations. So I cut the dose down slightly, kept giving it to you twice daily, and hoped that your malaise was just a temporary glitch in your recovery. At times it seemed that your energy level did pick up, even while getting two doses per day. Your pep, however, seemed more related to how much your hips hurt, and once we allowed them adequate time to recover, you seemed happier. Cindy frequently admonished me for working you too hard, or for not putting the brakes on your natural energy, but I always thought the more exercise, the better.

Certainly, in the last weeks of your life, at least, Cindy made a believer out of me. But, in the last week, all you wanted to do was rest, and no amount of rest seemed to make you feel any better. To us, your decline seemed very precipitous, like you had hit a wall. You had always seemed especially weak within a few hours of getting your DDAVP. As you remained on the medication, the period of weakness became longer and longer until it never went away. I became convinced that DDAVP was both your savior and your executioner.

When faced with the choice of saving your bladder and saving you during the last week, I naturally chose to save you. But either the medication was not the problem and something else was, or withdrawing the medication was too little too late. Why had I not reached this state of desperation earlier? Partly, because you had that wonderful day in the van while we watched Aida, and partly because you had shown excitement about going to the beach the Monday before the Friday we put you down. I finally changed my mind about the medication when I could no longer get you up in the evening. From the beginning, part of your bladder regimen involved taking you outside to urinate on an almost-every-two-hour schedule, at least while I was awake and at home. To achieve this schedule, both Cindy and I had come home from work over our lunch hours. However, you became increasingly unable to comply with this schedule. At first, I thought you were just getting lazy or that the arthritis in your hips made it difficult for you to rise from your position sprawled on your side. But as your wobbly gait and your vanishing stamina became more evident, I became convinced that a more generalized weakness caused all the false starts when you tried to walk your front legs straight and then struggled to make your hind legs work, before finally giving up. The final week, you stopped trying, and out of mercy, many times, I stopped trying. Only when I believed that the quality of your existence had deteriorated to a point that death became a viable option did I withdraw the mainstay of your lifeline.

I withheld the medication the Tuesday evening and Wednesday morning before the Friday we put you down. The only noticeable difference was a doubling of your urine volume in spite of minimal water intake and a doubling of the amount of time you had to endure the catheter. You planted yourself in one place, it seemed for hours, and resisted any extra movement. Your eyes especially were windows into your weariness. No intensity, no joy, so little interest. When I rushed home over the lunch hour to visit you, I wondered where you found the energy to move from the place that I had left you. But I was wrong to think that you could not get any weaker, because by Thursday, perhaps related to the final DDAVP dose that I had given you the evening before, you were incrementally weaker, like a very low tire that had gone almost completely flat.

Perhaps, with a minimal amount of blood testing, we could have determined more precisely why you were getting weak, in essence, why you were dying, and done something about it. Had you been a human patient of mine, I would have ordered these tests a couple weeks earlier to monitor for side effects from the medications, because we were still in a curative mode verses a comfort mode. But, in your case, I looked at it this way: there was no way we could maintain you without the DDAVP; we had already reached our limit with what we could practically do to keep you alive, giving you pills, giving you shots, taking you outside to urinate all the time, running home from work, catheterizing you, and fretting over many medical micromanagement decisions; if treating a side effect to the medication required any more work, time, and stress, we simply could not have withstood it. Up until the final week, the medications only seemed to be slowing you down, an acceptable side effect when compared to the way in which they seemed to give you back your life. By the last week, you were so ill that it would have required a major intervention, probably hospitalization, to correct all that was wrong, if it were even possible. Early in this final week, I also had my epiphany that I could only do so much for you, that the physiology of your organs had to bear most of the burden of keeping you alive and giving you some quality of life. After the epiphany, to those who inquired about you at the office, I half-jokingly referred to you as my hospice dog, because, in my more reasonable moments, I was beginning to let go. Periodically, I had switched to a mode of keeping you comfortable rather than extending your life. Nevertheless, I ruminated endlessly on what I could do to miraculously turn things around, or on what I could have done differently. I did not take myself off the hook then, and I have not taken myself off the hook yet. Still, I could find no practical reason to do blood work.

Cindy had read an article during your final month that said, "You (the pet owner) will know when it's time to put your dog down," and the words apparently stuck with her as gospel. Her imagination afforded her the luxury of planning the good life for you until one day she realized that the humane thing to do was to put you out of your misery. Her vision went from optimistic daylight to realistic nightfall. In many ways, she was helped by her ability to adjust to your progressive infirmities by viewing them as the natural consequences of aging rather than connecting them to a process that took you by steps closer to death, removing one reason after another for living. I may have helped in her final natural transition, but I think that her naiveté (focusing on life until the grim reaper was in the room) and her maintenance of an appropriate distance from the minute-by-minute fluctuations in your well-being were mostly responsible for her journey to your end. She had not allowed herself as much as I had to become immersed in the gray morass of the hour-by-hour changes in your pain and energy. She did not speculate why, at a given moment, you could not urinate or why it took you so long to go from lying to sitting. She did not rate your urine stream with the precision of an Olympic ice-skating judge. She did not as I did wish that a hard lump on the surface of your abdomen was the tip of the iceberg of a malignant process about which nothing could be done. As long as there was something potentially correctible, she did not feel the need as I did to try and manage it. She was not so enmeshed with you during your final weeks that she rode the roller coaster of your illness with its turns, dips, steep declines, and thrilling elevations. She did not live in my world of progressively darkening grays when one day the shade of gray became so dark, it became time to completely shut off the light. In the end, we came to the same place at the same time, but she stayed on the relatively level, high pass until the end, whereas I got lost in the valleys and then climbed back to the heights a few times before taking the bumpy, undulating decline with you.

****

I wore my heart on the sleeve of my white coat during your final days. Steeling myself for the inevitable, I began to gather advice about how deep I would need to bury you. To some extent, gathering this advice was merely a charade to hide in practical concerns the depth of my true feelings about you. Nevertheless, I did eventually get some helpful information, mixed in with well-intended, but potentially backbreaking advice. Many of my patients, mainly the dog lovers, had already met you in the foreground of the woodland snow pictures that Cindy took and hung in my windowless rooms to give me a view of the great outdoors. One fatherly patient with whom I had shared your saga of catheterizations asked me how you were doing. He had put down a couple of family dogs himself and buried them in his yard. He understood the depth of my feelings and in his ingenuous way was able to empathize with me without fanning my sorrow, for a moment reversing the roles of patient and healer. He had buried smaller dogs in more shallow graves, but when he heard that I would by burying you on the edge of acres of woods, he suggested burying you about six feet deep. He must have worried about my soft hands and slight physique because he suggested that I hire a couple of yard workers. His recommendation about the depth coincided with the one I had received from my veterinarian, so while I found the prospect daunting, I planned on it. However, I never considered hiring the job out. I consoled myself with the thought that the effort would be cathartic.

The most useful advice, I received was from my partner who lived on many acres in the country and boarded horses. He worked nearby in the rooms on the opposite hallway and did his patient charting 15 feet away, standing at his dictation cubbyhole opposite mine. Though we shared a practice together, our lives rarely intersected on a personal level, but this was the sort of practical problem that dipped into the core of his strength.

I asked in an offhanded way, "Hey, have you even had to bury a dog,"

"Yes, he said, "We buried Blackie and before that Winston." I detected no evidence of grief.

For a moment, I felt bad that I knew nothing about them. It seemed everyone knew about you, but I pursued it further, "Were they big dogs?"

"Blackie was a German shepherd and Winston was a Black Lab. I'd say that they were both about a hundred pounds."

I knew about his farm equipment from his farm stories that were his favorite, second only to adventures with his computers, so I said, "You're lucky. You had a backhoe to do your work."

"No." he said, taking no offense. "We save the backhoe for the horses. I dug the graves for the dogs myself." He was facing me now and had stopped arranging charts on his desk. We were officially having a conversation, and the two nurses who shared the workstation with us in the narrow transecting aisle were listening in.

"Did you dig the hole yourself?" He looked healthy enough with big enough pectorals, but aside from the vague sense that he was a geek, I recalled one too many stories about the untimely death of his family members to picture him digging six-foot holes.

"Sure. It takes just a few hours." There was no hint of bragging; it was just a definite recollection, which I found reassuring.

"How deep did you dig the holes?" I asked.

"About waist high." He stopped and measured, putting his hand just above his waist. "What is that? About three or four feet?"

"Didn't you worry about wild animals digging up such a shallow grave?" I do not know why I preferred maggots to wild animals, but it would have been the ultimate disrespect to you to allow living carnivores to drag your dead bones to the four winds.

"That should be plenty deep for an animal that size. We didn't have any problems."

"But we plan to bury our dog in the woods." From holiday parties at his place, I remembered acres of open fields to which I did not think a "wild" animal would expose itself.

"We put Blackie near the edge of the woods. No animals disturbed his grave"

I turned this new possibility over for a few silent moments; then I said, "It just doesn't seem that there will be all that much dirt on top of him. By the time you put him in the hole—he's a foot or so thick— there will only be a couple of feet on top of him."

"He won't be a foot after you put all that dirt on him."

The nurses who were listening collectively gasped at his last comment. However coldhearted and blunt it was on the surface, it was intended as a purely practical comment. I appreciated his logic. He reassured me enough that I eventually dug a four-foot hole and tamped you down further with the two-hundred- pound root ball of a seven-foot dogwood. Still I facetiously thanked him for sharing that image with me.

By the time I had this conversation with my partner, your fate had already been sealed. It was Friday morning, October 13th; you were still alive, but barely. Cindy had taken a sick day off from school and was staying with you while I worked my half-day. Your deterioration had prompted us to call the veterinarian the day before to make tentative plans to end your misery. Only some improvement in your status would have given you a stay of execution. When your condition had worsened overnight, I reluctantly confirmed a time with your veterinarian, for about 5:30 that evening, or after she completed office hours. Mercifully, she agreed to come to you because you were in no condition to get to her.

Our willing decision to set a time to end the life of a breathing, sentient creature so loved and part of us seems both amazing and masochistic. We euphemistically call it euthanasia, a dirty word for humans, but humane when it comes to pets. We set the time of death in some states for the execution of the most heinous murderers, but that is in the name of human justice, not humanity. Humanity might dictate a lifetime of remedial imprisonment. We schedule risky surgeries that might result in death, but these are intended to either improve the quality or quantity of life, or both. We know that our human loved ones are going to die soon, but we never know, in the absence of Kevorkian, the exact hour or minute they will be no more. Yet, with our animals we impose this time of death on our innocent companions, with mercy in our hearts. In the end, it is our humanity that allows us to make such painful decisions. Still, waiting for the hour or minute of your last breath was like waiting to have my heart cut out without Novocain.

****

When the week started, I knew that your days were getting short, but I had no idea that you were entering your last week. Cindy was cloaked in optimism and was still making plans that included you eight months hence. Yet, there was something that we both saw in you that caused us to arrive in unison at the painful decision to set a time to end your life if it did not end on its own. Your weakness had progressed so that you could barely go from lying to standing, much less walk the hallway and descend the three front porch steps to urinate and have an outdoor bowel movement. This state was not a temporary setback; your sun was beginning to dip below the horizon. I had jarred Cindy from her steadfast optimism earlier that week, but still she had no idea you were so ill until she came home over her lunch break the Thursday before the final Friday. I had already been home and managed to get you out the front door where you urinated on the wraparound porch, and then, to my dismay, out of habit, walked down the steps. You managed to get up the steps, hesitating at the bottom like the weight lifter who must mentally prepare himself before he snatches five hundred pounds. You stumbled through the doorway and made it 20 feet to the rug in the kitchen where you collapsed and sprawled on your side.

That is where Cindy found you during her lunch visit. You acknowledged her presence with a slight lift of your head, but you otherwise lay there lifeless. What struck and horrified her the most was your eye. Though she did not recall it at the time, she had seen an eye like yours one other time on our oldest white cat, Whinny. Both cats and dogs have a third eyelid hidden in the inner corner of the eye. Usually it sweeps undetectably across the eye like a windshield wiper. However, in Whinny's case for a week or so, and in your case during the last two days of your life, the eyelid did not retract back to its place of hiding. It formed a grotesque, opaque, pus-colored film over at least half of your eye. To the uninitiated, it appeared that your eyeball had rotated around in the eye socket and revealed the back of it. The eye looked useless, until on close inspection, one could see the partially shrouded pupil following the activity within its view. You lay lifeless from your previous exertions with your good eye down, deaf already to our comings and goings, turning the frightening eye on Cindy. That is when the horror struck her and she knew.

That evening, your condition and the conclusion we had both drawn were the first words from our mouths. I called your veterinarian to make tentative plans for the next day, but I still held out hope that one of two things might happen. Maybe you would make a miraculous turnaround, but I knew this to be unlikely. What I hoped for even more, because it seemed possible, was that you would die without our assistance, that I would fall asleep and when I awakened you would be gone, or that one of the times when I strained to hear your breathing in the darkness, I would find absolute silence.

I had conjured a couple of scenarios in my own mind that were quickly terminal. In the last week as you lay enervated, frequently, I put my head to your chest to determine how your heart was holding up under the stress of your illness. Many times, I found it beating rapidly and erratically; with your weakness, it seemed possible that your heart was responsible for your lost stamina and that it would just give out. I never confirmed my impression with a stethoscope. I did not want to weaken my hope that your heart would take you naturally.

Also, I formulated an alternative theory for your

weakness. One of your less becoming, rarely used nicknames in your latter years was "Lumpy." You always had this mat of blond and red Dennis the Menace fur to go along with his personality, but as you aged, embedded in this fur were soft lumps of all sizes. You had a fingertip-sized cyst at the base of your left ear, a particularly protrusive one on your chest, a half-fist-sized one on your right leg, and another soft fatty one on your abdomen. What I thought I discovered in your last week was one in your abdomen that was harder than the others, and less superficial. I tried to wrap my fingers around it to find the base of it; I nearly convinced myself that it extended into the abdominal cavity and originated from a major abdominal organ. I was hopeful enough about it that I mentioned it to your veterinarian. Before she gave you your final injection, she asked about the lump. She quickly dismissed it as a superficial lump like all your others. After your vet's terminal potion had had its intended effect, I re-examined your lump in the relaxed muscles of your abdominal wall; how could I have been so stupid? What kind of doctor was I? She was right; it was superficial like all the others. But I had wanted a natural death so badly, some cause for it that was out of my control, that my imagination tried to turn it into something it was not.

When you did not do us the kindness of dying on your own, I believed that you just wanted to stay with us until the end. I believed that even in your perilously weakened state that the pleasure you received from our company outweighed the grip of death. These motives that I ascribed to you only made it more difficult to put you out of your misery.

In response to the absolute finite time that remained for you, Cindy and I decided to stay at your side on the carpet in the living room throughout your last night. Neither of us slept well under camping conditions, even indoors on the living room carpet, but lost sleep was a minor sacrifice for you. We catheterized you late that evening in the hope that we would rid you of any urge to empty your bladder. We hoped that we could eliminate any further need for you to strain yourself.

The night seemed to be going well for you until around 3 AM when I heard you stirring. A couple of times, you raised yourself from your sprawled position on your side to a lying position on your abdomen with your head up. You panted gently in the way that made it seem you were smiling and happy. At first, I thought that awakening was your way of recognizing our efforts to spend the night with you and you were doing your best to spend some quality time with us. However, you had already erased my illusions about this panting smile. Many times I had seen you transition from an exhausted state to this smiling pant. I had assumed that it meant that you were feeling better, until one time after I catheterized your overloaded bladder, you immediately sunk back into a sound exhausted sleep. When I re-examined all the other times you wore this panting smile, I realized that many times it had occurred under similar circumstances. Your gentle panting smiles signaled mounting discomfort with your bladder.

I moved to you to reciprocate your efforts to spend time with me; no matter that we were in the middle of the middle of the night. I ran my hand along your nose and across the sharp ridge of the crown of your head. I inquired if there was anything that I could do for you. You did not immediately respond, because you lacked the strength to follow through on your urges. But to my amazement, and dismay, you made the motions to try and get up. I did not encourage you, at first, because I did not believe that you could make it to the front door. But you persisted, and I got up and said the words that I had said hundreds of times before, "Do you need to go outside." It was a phrase that had no trouble penetrating your deafness and meant specifically, "Do you need to urinate outside?"

You stood stiff legged like a rickety old chair occupied by a full-grown man. When you made it to the hallway wood floor, you walked like someone on skates for the first time. You wove down the hall, barely making it over the lip of the braided rug. You stopped; you started; you almost fell. You made it all the way to the threshold of the open front door and then you collapsed. There we sat, while you blocked the door wide open, watching a howling November gale that descended upon South Haven six weeks early.

At first, I thought that you could not have picked a worse place to collapse. A few feet earlier or a few later, I could have closed the door. But then I decided to settle down beside you and wait, and imagined that we were the only ones awake in South Haven, stuck in our doorway watching the wind and rain transform the woodland night, immersing ourselves in it as it tossed the leafy heads of monstrous trees, power-sprayed the holly bushes along the front porch, blasted us with wind chills that rivaled leafless snowy nights, soaked every outdoor nook and cranny like a dishwasher, and roared in waves like a 10-foot Lake Michigan surf. I was in awe of your will and courage, creating stories until the very end. I did not know when or if you would rise from that spot, but contentment was replacing my concern. A mild night would have been easier, but a wild night was an exclamation mark on your life.

You did not allow me to relax for long. You struggled to your feet and continued on your original mission. You stepped out onto the deck of the front porch, and squatted to urinate. Perhaps, out of habit, I watched to see if anything came out, but I thought that attempt would be the end of your efforts and that you would have the sense to come back inside. Instead, striking horror and astonishment in my heart, you walked down the steps and turned on the bark path that ran the length of our front porch. Not only had you walked down the steps that I was sure you could not ascend, but now you had disappeared into the howling drenched darkness of the middle of the night. The darkness swallowed you from sight and the wind's havoc from earshot. What the hell were you thinking? What the hell was I thinking? You were going to die out there, because I was not going to be able to find you and if I did, I was not going to be able to get you back in. Maybe you would die on your own accord after all. Now that would be a story to tell.

I watched for a few moments to see if you would reappear into the front floodlight. Then I got my raincoat and went out to look for you. I walked in the direction I had seen you head. I had not been looking for very long when I found you on the side of the house between the wraparound porch and the rhododendrons that crowded it. Why in your weakened state you had taken this ridiculous obstacle-laden route, I never did figure out. Maybe you were more delirious or demented than I thought. It was not the first time, but it would be the last. The rhododendron shoots had taken your feet from under you and you lay there. We were no more than thirty feet from the front door, but it felt like you were entangled in the undergrowth deep of a temperate rainforest.

I could wake up Cindy, I thought, and perhaps the two of us could squeeze behind the sprawling, dripping rhododendron and lift you and carry you inside. Perhaps, we could maneuver you onto a blanket and carry you. But somehow, I reasoned, you had made it this far; all I had to do was guide you along the shortest, easiest path out of this mess, past the rhododendrons and through the clearing between the holly bushes in front and the honeysuckle on the corner of the wraparound porch. You might stumble over the small boulders and the euonymus groundcover in the clearing, but it was easier than turning you around and going back the way you had come. I took a commanding, desperate hold on the loop in your choke collar and you got to your feet with surprising ease. You stumbled through the path, but you did not fall. You angled up the front porch steps, taking one at a time. I did not let go of your collar until I had you safely inside. I do not know if you ever did urinate, but that was going to be our last adventure outside with you while you were alive.

****

That night ended early the next morning. Recalling the reason for our outdoor adventure, I awakened Cindy shortly after six AM to catheterize you. We drained over three-fourths quart of urine from you, probably twice the volume you had consumed in the last 24 hours. That was the way your body functioned without DDAVP. In a last ditch effort to revive you, I had withdrawn all your medications, without success. Sticking to my routine, I did my morning stretching exercises and took a shower, rinsing away the sleepless night. I could now leave you in good conscience. Cindy, my surrogate, the middle note in our triad, remained by your side so that I could temporarily depart our all-encompassing, all consuming island and enter the mainland of my existence.

The surface of my morning was routine, with the exception of my conversation with my partner about the specifics of dog burial. Though I started with a half day, my practical self anticipated my needs and closed my schedule as soon as I arrived. The events of the night, though offering minimal sleep, had left my senses acutely alive as if the immersion mode of our nocturnal island had ferried over into the more mundane realm of my life. The interactions with my patients flowed with unusual empathy and humor. In spite of my weary mind, I spoke coherently in unusually flowing paragraphs, adjusting my language to my audience of one. Your situation moved to the background until I had seen my last patient. Only slowly did you leak back in. I still had messages to which I had to respond and a few abnormal labs to take care of. I began to feel my weariness and began to move in slow motion. The leak went from a trickle to a steady stream. My work began to falter. Then the floodgates opened. You were still breathing. What I was doing here suddenly seemed unimportant, something that could wait. You could not wait. This was my last afternoon with you, "my last afternoon," a phrase absolute and definitive and yet pregnant with the unknown. What it did mean was that you absolutely "would" not be around for more than a few hours. What your indefinite physical absence would feel like, I had only the vaguest notion. There was this certainty, this awful certainty, finally, climaxing a period of awful uncertainty. I knew that I had to jump off the precipice, but would I crash on the rocks below or glide to a soft landing on a sandbar? There was no turning back.

I arrived home to find you still lying in the living room. You acknowledged my return home with a meaningful, but infinitesimal fraction of your former energy. You did not come charging down the hallway and slide the last ten feet into me, nearly knocking me over. You merely lifted your head in my direction and caught a glimpse of me with your partially shrouded eye. You no longer had the energy to wag your tail, part of your greeting even the week before. Subdued light from skies still frowning from the previous day's storm crept through the western wall of picture windows. CNN droned in the background and added its fluctuating unnatural light. The room was not quite gloomy, but solemn. A day with brilliant sun would have seemed incongruous like a funeral dirge in c-major. From the hallway, I could see that nothing had changed to alter the course of our plan.

I had five or six precious, tormented hours left with you when I arrived home shortly after noon. You were not suffering terribly, but you had no life. Your living presence still embodied the warmth and joy of our bond, but the activities that created the bond were almost all but in the past; there was only a wisp of a future. You still seemed to take pleasure in my company, expending what little energy you had to take my little gifts of food, but even indulging this, your most instinctual instinct, your food obsession, was a mighty struggle. I still had the greatest respect for your gift, but I would carry that with me whether you were here or in an eternal elsewhere. I was not struggling with my decision to put you down. I was in pain; your dying presence was the last ember of the joy you had brought to my life and I was about to experience the loss of that in a way that would take me some time to understand. I knew that I was powerless to turn the clock back, but I had not yet given up on keeping time still, living in that afternoon as long as I wanted, feeding you bits of cheese and roast beef, and sniffing the unique fresh canine smell of your fur that was you to me, that smell I wanted to brand in my memory forever.

Cindy gave me the position near your head during most of your remaining hours, because she had spent the morning with you while I worked. Neither of us left your presence for more than a moment. I went to the refrigerator a few times, first so that you could finish the roast beef in which I had wrapped your pills for the previous two weeks. Lying on your side, you snapped up the meaty treats with more gusto than I expected. When you finished with the roast beef, I brought back slices of Jarlsburg cheese and fed it in bits to you. I angled a shallow bowl of water so that you could lap the water from the side of your mouth while I supported your head. It was sloppy but effective.

I had always imagined one sure sign that a pet was dying

was that it stopped eating, but you ate until the very end. I should not have been surprised, because you loved food more than life. For weeks you lacked the enthusiasm of your former days, but you almost always ate. Your gusto for food on your last afternoon was reminiscent of your uncontained enthusiasm for your everyday dog food, especially in the morning when I was still shaking off sleep. You would rear back on your hind legs and then lunge forward, driving your nose into the top of the dog food bag, marvelously impatient, and I could not help but laugh inside and say out loud, "Show me what you want!" And you would shove your nose into the bag a half dozen more times and seemingly throw your head in the direction of your food bowl to show me more explicitly what you wanted me to do with your food. I could not help but taunt you a little bit, because that simple act of driving your nose into the bag was better than a pot of coffee in the morning.

As you ate and drank, I became concerned that you might rally and try and get up like the night before. To eliminate any uncomfortable urges from a full bladder, Cindy and I catheterized you one last time of over a pint of urine. We had to turn you over to accomplish this; you let out a frightened, pained yelp that hurt us more than we hurt you. After draining your bladder, we did not have the heart to turn you back the other way; this left your partly cloudy eye up.

Once, when I left to go to the bathroom, Cindy told me when I returned that you had lifted your head and watched me leave the room. I was profoundly touched by this gesture. We were still the center of your universe, the gods in whom you put all your trust. You did not spend your last hours comatose; you seemed compelled to remain alert for this special time with us, even as you lay dying. This minor gesture would come back to haunt me. Several hours later, I was disturbed when you became rigid briefly in my arms from the pain of an injection into the muscle of your leg. A couple days went by before I recognized why this flinch before the end left me so uneasy. When you had used your last bit of energy to watch me, it had become a symbolic gesture for your trust in me. When I took you in my arms and allowed someone to surprise you with a painful injection, no matter how necessary, I felt that I had betrayed that trust. I had more trouble with the method of delivery of the medication than its action. The flinch added an element of unexpected violence to a process that I had implicitly promised you would be peaceful and painless.

The anticipation of the unknown wound a spring in my gut as time whittled away at the afternoon. Cindy had given away her seven-year-old black lab when it became too aggressive in defending her from our seven-month-old toddler. She grieved him for days, but was reassured months later when she found him fatter and happy, lying beside his new master, an older man with a wife disabled by Parkinson's disease. In the last year, I had watched my father die in a 12-hour period after a stroke, but as the physician in charge of some of the aspects of his care, I did not feel as helpless or lost. Also, my relationship with him over the decades had evolved from one of dependency to rebellious independence to a healthy and satisfying interdependence. Even before he died, I had learned both to live without him and to carry him in my heart. The only pet that we ever did put down was a kitten that broke its back hiding in the wheel-well of a moving car. But we had never put down a pet with which we had the full life cycle to develop a mature bond. I lived in these final moments in this tension between doing the mundane things you needed and enjoyed, bringing you food and being with us, and knowing that I would have to face the moment when you would become suddenly lifeless. If given the choice of putting you down or jumping into ice water, I would have taken the polar bear swim, and I hate cold water. So here I arrive at my fully developed metaphor for the anticipation I felt that afternoon, using the precipice and cold water; it was like standing at the precipice overlooking an Alaskan glacial lake, knowing that at a certain hour we had no choice but to jump into the breathtaking ice water. Cindy and I could swim ashore; you would not. Odd, had you died spontaneously, I would have grieved as hard, but missed the anticipation of the swim.

****

Your veterinarian's busy day at the clinic gave us a forty-five minute reprieve, but she finally arrived shortly before six carrying everything she needed in her traditional doctor's black bag. Somehow, I thought she would be towing a cart or carrying a large metal suitcase to house the instruments of an act so final. She had only a black bag. It also might seem paradoxical that she used one of the time-honored symbols of the healing arts to carry the potions that ended your life. But if one of the goals of the healing arts is to relieve misery, when there is no hope, the act of euthanasia intersects with the humanity of the healing arts. So I will not from this point forward associate the black bag with the duties of the grim reaper.

By the time she arrived with her black bag, we were ready. If nothing else, the purgatory of the last twelve hours had prepared us for this moment. Your veterinarian did not disrupt the gravity and solemnity in the room with idle chitchat. Nor did she attempt to offer the solacing words of a Rabbi or minister. She was solemn and business like. She remembered my concern about your abdominal tumor, and quickly felt it and dashed one of my alternative theories for your rapid demise. Then she took what she needed from her black bag and explained what was going to happen. She would first give you an injection to relax you and put you asleep so that you would not struggle when she injected the lethal dose of anesthesia in your vein. She warned us that you might feel some discomfort from the injection. She explained that the lethal dose of anesthesia, 12 cc of Succinylcholine worked by stopping your heart and breathing. We put a chuck beneath your hindquarters after she told us that it was not uncommon to defecate when the paralytic agent relaxed all the muscles.

There was no drum roll after her explanation. She injected your hip with the sleeping agent. You tensed briefly with the injection, but after no more than thirty seconds, your body completely relaxed, so much so that your tongue slid from your mouth. She put a tourniquet around one of your front legs to engorge a vein. Then, with surprising ease, she inserted the needle of a large syringe into the vein, released the tourniquet, and pulled back on the syringe. A flush of your blood confirmed that she was in your vein, and then, she emptied the contents of the syringe into your vein. You were already so relaxed that there was no obvious change. She waited a couple of minutes and then put her stethoscope to your chest to confirm that you had no heartbeat. I accepted her offer to use her stethoscope to listen for myself. After all, I practiced the healing arts as well and I was going to have to live with the absence of your heartbeat the rest of my life.

She did not stay for more than a couple of minutes after this. She did not seem to be in a hurry. There just was not much to say. She merely reassured us that we had done everything that we could have done. We thanked her as profusely as we could for going out of her way to euthanize a living note in the triad of our home. I walked her to the door and let her out. When I closed the behind her and turned toward the living room, the house was vast, silent, and empty.

I did not feel the pain at first, even as you went limp and your heart silenced. I did not feel relief either, like one is supposed to feel when a loved one dies after a long drawn-out illness. Something had changed though, because I felt alone with Cindy, like the house had just grown larger because the life in it had shrunk. I could sense as well that I would need to make a small adjustment of being with her without you to care for. You had been our raison d'être and now you were gone. I had already sobbed in my anticipation of this moment, but I still thought that there might be some tears of anguish to come. But maybe not. I suppose that I was in a hiatus of sensation, like one experiences after he stubs his toe and at first feels nothing. Yet, he knows that he jammed that toe hard into the leg of the chair and that he must wait a second or two for the sensation to travel to his brain before he learns how bad the damage was. I was still waiting for the pain to reach my brain. As it would turn out, I had broken my toe.

When the pain did hit, it felt like my chest was not nearly large enough to contain it all. It came in a huge wave that arose in my gut and crashed in my chest, and then beat me up to get out. All I could do was shudder under its force and release some of it in streams of tears. I remember thinking that I might get relief by vomiting some of the grief that was crashing ashore in me. For a moment, I felt that there was nothing or no one on earth that could console me. Cindy was there, more to me than life itself, but this grief was so huge that it not only filled me, but also surrounded me like a mote and would not let anyone in. It stranded me in a vast sunless universe feeling utterly alone and helpless. Even now, recollecting this ridiculous emotional pain, one hundred pages into purging and understanding it, I still feel so small and embarrassed. (No offense, Izzy, but you are just a dog.)

****

In the calmer and rational troughs between the waves, Cindy and I began to prepare for your burial. Cindy had suggested that we bury you on your bed, but I objected because it would take up too much room in your grave. Simultaneously, we arrived at using the sheet that for years had projected the sofa from your sandpapery paws. We did decide to use your bed to transport you, however, from the living room to the back screened-in porch where it became you intermediate resting place. You had maintained your dignity even in death— you did not defecate and Lord knows you did not urinate in your ultimate relaxation. Together, we moved you onto your cedar stuffed bed that you wore out only after you could no longer hop into our bed. I then dragged the bed with you on it over the oak plank floors of the kitchen to the back porch where we had spent the long night together six weeks earlier. This time you would not pace.

The early evening was November-cold and blustery and twilight dark from the overcast. I imagined the outdoor cold would keep you as fresh as the refrigeration kept my father while we waited for his funeral. The screen would keep away the predators. We would not be there to keep you company, but you would be safe all alone out there. We both gave you long hugs before leaving you. You were still warm and had your distinctive Izzy scent that I inhaled like the perfume of a lover. I felt the sharp ridge along the crown of your head one more time. You seemed at least as large in death as you did in life. I had no illusions embracing you; you already felt no more alive than a solid stuffed animal and returned nothing to my embrace. But I was not going to leave you out there all night and then for eternity without hugging you again. When we re-entered the kitchen and closed the door behind us,

Cindy and I both looked at you through the window of the door. We were still impressed by how majestic and beautiful you were stretched out on your bed.

I turned next to digging your grave, using whatever light was still available to me. Cindy, recognizing the solitary nature of my task, decided to restock the house with food and went to the grocery. I measured your stretched out corpse so that I could dig a grave that would not crowd your limbs. When I circumscribed the grave on the northwestern edge of our yard, I added several inches in both directions for your head and legs. I began digging like I was running a race, trying to give an effort worthy of your gift. I was not merely digging a hole; you were going to hallow this ground. I threw the dirt to the far northwestern edge, separating the topsoil from the sandy subsoil and keeping the edge nearest the house clear for your approach. When I felt my muscles begin to tire and ache, I used the letters of your name, I-z-z-y, as my mantra, throwing a shovel of dirt with each letter, going through at least three Izzy cycles before taking a rest, losing myself in the restive trees, the fresh turned-earth aroma, and the coming night. Cindy's headlights shone brightly when she returned from the grocery. From the window in the kitchen, she would watch me finish your grave the following morning. But that night, I blended into the night, like you once did when you left the lighted porch to walk away your discomfort.

After Cindy retrieved me from your grave and brought me back into the house, I set about putting away everything that would remind me of your illness. Your illness had been a wonderful glue and a rite of passage into a sort of transient Garden of Eden, but it was the result that I wanted to remember, not the cause. I did not throw the paraphernalia away; I merely put it out of sight—the box of catheters, syringes, basin, and paper towels— downstairs in the unfinished side of the basement; the medications with my meticulous flow sheet, I put in a crowded cabinet in my study. Clearing your sick equipment from the living areas may not have occurred to me had I not seen my mom soon after my father died going through all of his clothes. She kept a few articles of clothing that had fond memories associated with them, but she gave the rest to us, her children, and what we did not want, to Goodwill. At the time, I thought that she was clearing his things out too soon, but admired her for facing up to it. Had I not witnessed her courage, I might have been inclined to keep your things in view, painful as they were, to help keep your presence alive rather than move on. By the time we went to bed that night, the only reminder that remained were a few fur balls from your coat that concentrated along the walls in the hallway. That night, Cindy and I found sleep in each other's arms without the comfort of your rhythmic heavy breathing.

The following morning, I rose early to finish digging your grave. Passing through the back porch, your temporary resting place, I noticed a small pool of blood around your head that had not been there the evening before. Briefly, I considered the possibility that your heart resumed pumping to cause such a thing. But your body was cold and stiff from the night chill. The explanation was much less magical. When rigor mortis set in, your worn teeth clamped down on the piece of tongue that hung from your mouth. Briefly I chided myself for not recognizing this possibility because I had seen your veterinarian push your tongue back in your mouth after she sedated you. As a result of my negligence, I had another unsavory memory to defuse.

The remainder of the work on your grave went quickly because we lived on an old Lake Michigan dune field. After removing the first foot or so of topsoil and roots, I encountered only a stray small trunk of a root before reaching nearly pure sand. You would eventually lie on a bed of yellowish-orange sand, returning more organic substance to this layer of the dune than it had seen in centuries. The yard sloped to the northwest making the hole over waist high on the near edge and just under waist high on the far side. As the hole became deeper, I began to have difficulty heaving the sand from the bottom of it over the growing mound of sand on the far edge of the grave; in some cases, for each shovelful I threw out, a small avalanche slid back in. At this point, I decided to refine the hole into a chamber or a tomb. The walls were as vertical as I could make them; the bottom edges were squarer than they really needed to be; and the bed was as level as eyeballing could make it. The aesthetically pleasing geometry of your grave reflected the need that makes others choose fine cherry caskets for their recently lost loved ones.

    I climbed out of the grave much like someone gets out of the deep end of a swimming pool, supporting all my weight on my hands and shoulders, and then carefully throwing my leg up over the edge while thrusting my body up by straightening my elbows. It disturbed me when a small portion of the top edge collapsed from the movement and fell to the bottom of the grave. Each subsequent time I had to exit the grave, I moved my hands further from the edge and pushed up with the greatest force I could muster to avoid such tiny accidents. This was the irrational state of my mind as I prepared to permit the second law of thermodynamics increase the disorder in what was formerly your beautiful, naughty living body and personality maintained by biological processes. I was trying to maintain control where I could when Nature was really in control.

****

Once your grave was completely prepared, Cindy and I felt comfortable leaving you while we sought a dogwood tree to plant as a grave marker and memorial to you. The night before, we had decided upon a dogwood because we both had fond memories of our bygone days in North Carolina when dogwood blossoms heralded the arrival of spring on mountainsides of barely clad trees. We knew just where the perfect one must exist, even this late in the planting season, at a nursery in Glenn, Michigan, that was as much an arboretum as it was a depot for landscaping needs. We discovered the place a few weeks earlier during its late season sale. We had created a need for new and different plants in our wilderness garden when we had cleared sassafras and oaks from the woods of our side yard. Our salesperson during this first visit was engaging, friendly, and knowledgeable, and he seemed extraordinarily intimate with all of his plants; he was as much a naturalist as he was a salesman. One of our main criteria for plant selection during our first trip was that they did not appear on the menu of deer. Another was that they could not grow as tall as their predecessors, blocking the sun from flowering shrubs and ornamental trees. He must have been familiar with the first restriction from previous sales. When I migrated toward juniper shrubs and Michigan holly that seemed to meet the second criterion, he said emphatically, "Nope. Deer candy." That term, "deer candy" sure seemed to make deer eating habits less irascible. After all, who could blame them for chowing down on a pot full of ungulate sweets? So we returned home with plants that were not our first choices, but were among the last for deer. You watched me plant them during one of your final weekends, the waxy bayberry that might one day block the view of our compost from the kitchen window, and the Vibernum and red maple that might one day block the view of our western neighbor. Struggling with the heavy root ball of the red maple would prepare me for handling your memorial tree.

The Saturday morning before your burial was the gusty, chilly tail of the preceding stormy days. We drove down the long entrance road of the nursery, through woods of mature trees that terminated in a small circular gravel parking lot. The road was so long and the woods so dense that the parking lot and the nursery seemed almost intentionally hidden, instilling it with an element of beauty and mystery like Shangri La. We arrived to an empty parking lot; the stormy aftermath had created an opportunity for us by frightening everyone else off temporarily. We were Noah's doves at the Wavecrest Nursery that morning. The only problem was that the place, still littered with branches, many thicker in diameter than my arm, seemed so empty that we were not sure anyone was working the nursery. But we found "Deer Candy" keeping warm inside the small store near the parking lot. For my grieving heart, "Deer Candy" was an uplifting presence.

"Deer Candy" accompanied us, first on foot and then on a golf cart, like he had nothing else in the world that he would rather be doing. Only a single phone call interrupted the attention that he gave us, and no other customers arrived until we were loading up our van. The nursery was full of his flora children and he had at least a notion where every one was or had been, so he had no trouble locating the dogwoods spread out over the entire grounds. The grounds were not divided, as best I could tell, into simple segregated neighborhoods, dogwoods with dogwoods, junipers with junipers, maples with maples, bigger trees with bigger trees, and smaller ones with smaller ones. They seemed to be arranged in aesthetically pleasing groups, broadleaf trees with nice hemlocks, with fountains and granite benches interspersed, and paths winding between. The root balls enclosed in wire baskets were buried, giving each grouping a sense of permanence. Knowing just where a tree was required a familiarity with each of the more significant trees. The depth of his relationship with the more significant trees was evident in his disappointment when he found that a tree was missing, after preparing us to meet the tree of our dreams.

"I know that I still have a couple of nice dogwoods left," he said, after he found the first one missing. He had that way of taking ownership of the establishment, speaking without pretension in the first person singular, though we learned later that he only worked there, for seven years. He showed us two types of dogwoods, one that he called a Kousa dogwood and the other, the kind with which we were more familiar, the flowering dogwood. He had suspiciously more Kousa dogwoods to show us than flowering dogwoods. The Kousa were hardy and full, but they lacked the characteristic shape of the North Carolina dogwood that made it so recognizable to me from a hundred yards. Rather than growing horizontally with layered branches like the flowering dogwood, the Kousa grew vertically with its branches spraying upwards. What's more, they were all loaded with unfamiliar berries, a waxy washed out version of red raspberries with much less flavor. He assured me that it had beautiful spring flowers like the flowering dogwood, but the flowers came after the tree leafed out. Some people like it one way and some the other. But our recollection of the North Carolina dogwood did not include leaves distracting us from the flowers. He eventually guided us to an island of trees that had a seven-foot flowering dogwood in its midst. Unlike the Kousa, it had lost its leaves with the exception of a few straggling brown ones, leaving much of its possibility to the imagination. When we showed only lukewarm interest, he decided to explore the "back nine" of the nursery that contained the trees-in-waiting, those that were intended to find new homes the next season.

We explored the back nine in a golf cart. I sat beside Deer Candy while Cindy sat in the back seat. Deer Candy was my height, probably older than the late-twenties boyish looks that his smooth pale skin and manicured brown hair gave him.

If not for regular close shaving he would have had a permanent five o'clock shadow. His eyes were light, green-blue or hazel; nothing was brown or deeply set that gave his face any seriousness. His carriage had an unpretentious jaunty grace to it, fit for a master of ceremony or a mountain guide. But mostly, he was defined by his manner, a gentle, informative, self-assured misfit who was completely comfortable among his flora children. He mothered his plants and the customer who shared his interest in mothering them. In my vulnerable state, I could not have been in better hands.

I felt privileged to be touring the grounds of this magnificent planned community of landscaping trees and plants, a Shangri la among nurseries. As we headed toward the back nine, the dark veil over the heavens began to open up in earnest. Big blue patches provided fairways for racing broken cumulous clouds. The air rushed by us, scoured and clean. The cart's movement created a tiny headwind, but the storm's aftermath sent a feistier cross current. Sitting in that golf cart, a portal mercifully opened to the infinite, temporarily accepting my grief and leaving me with a peace that was profound in contrast to the turbulence of the preceding days. During this calm hiatus, for the first time, I heard over the din of the wind-tossed trees the distant roar of semi trucks. I asked Deer Candy about it. I-196 was within earshot of our Shangri la. No matter. What I made of that moment existed in my mind, and I appreciated the intrusion of reality into this tiny peaceful eddy of my existence.

Deer Candy briefly climbed out of the golf cart to open the gate that separated the planned community of the front nine from the back nine. We entered a completely different neighborhood. Instead of aesthetically pleasing groups of plants on winding streets, there were large tracts of trees in rows, much like one would expect in a nursery. Dense woods surrounded the more open tracts, but the back nine contrasted with the front nine like an old upscale community with new suburban sprawl. We traveled almost to the northernmost part of the grounds before the cart turned west down an aisle. By then, I had grown as comfortable in the cart as one curled by a fire with a good book and a cup of hot chocolate. I had to force my muscles to work so that we could view a few more trees.

Once more, we found three Kousas for each nice flowering dogwood. Deer Candy finally found the flowering dogwood he had in mind. It was more symmetrical than the other on the front nine, just as tall, lots of buds for next year with the same straggling late fall leaves. Cindy and I considered this second tree with indecisive equanimity. Deer Candy had shown us two nice dogwoods, neither a gem nor a piece of coal. Deer Candy stepped in and made the decision for us. In spite of the extra effort he had made to take us to the back nine, he voiced a preference for the split trunk of the first tree to the symmetric single trunk of the latter. Cindy agreed and I was relieved to let them make the decision.

On our return trip to the front nine, having viewed the grounds, we focused more on Deer Candy. He told us about his winter job which was a perfect complement to outdoor landscaping, working for a company that decorated houses, sometimes for the rich and famous. Most of the time, he regaled us with his experience doing the Christmas decoration in the home of the wealthy Republican candidate for Michigan governor in November, Dick DeVos. Though he began by saying that he was a nice man, he concluded that he had too much wealth to possibly understand the plight of the ordinary citizen. He spent a year's salary, $25,000, decorating the house for a single day of the year. He owned nine houses and six yachts around the country, and he may have been at any one of them on Christmas day. Deer Candy was most impressed that DeVos employed a crew of painters year round to touch up the paint inside and outside the house. Mr. DeVos was rarely present while he prepared the house for Christmas, but his children were; he felt that they were so accustomed to strangers in the house that they treated him like he was part of the furniture. Still, he felt fortunate to have the job. And the paint crew probably would have reiterated this gratitude. But I think that we all agreed that he did not need another mansion, the governor's mansion. While we talked, the tree of your life and death grew another shoot—had we not pursued your memorial, we would not have heard any of Deer Candy's tales.

Loading the dogwood in the car was as much fun as it was an ordeal. At first, I was a spectator while Deer Candy and a co-worker, 20 years his senior but much more the woodsman, wrestled with the ball of the tree. At first, it seemed that Deer Candy was in charge because he seemed to give his co-worker what should have been the most laborious job, digging the root ball out of the ground. Meanwhile, Deer Candy bound the branches with twine to protect and compress them for their ride in the van. When his co-worker thought he had freed the root ball, he and Deer Candy grasped the handles of large metal hooks and embedded them in the root ball bound in a wire basket, and then tried to lift the ball out of its hole. You would have thought that they were trying to lift a semi. The tree did not budge a millimeter. I thought that Deer Candy's estimate for the root ball of 150 pounds underestimated its weight by threefold. But Deer Candy suggested in high spirits that if the root ball had been freed properly in the first place, they would not have had any trouble. In response, his co-worker dredged up a less than stellar performance Deer Candy had made when loading another tree. I got the distinct impression that some of their Laurel and Hardy routine was for my benefit. It went on for another 10 minutes while the co-worker dug around the tree with the shovel and the two of them tried to lift it out. Finally, Deer Candy took over the shovel and made his attempt to free the root ball. Then giving it all they had, they lifted it three inches before dropping it.

After watching the comedy act for a while, I finally offered to help, and Deer Candy found a hook for me. The three of us lifted the root from the hole and set it on the eight-by-eight retaining timber surrounding this cluster of trees. It was all high-spirited and satisfying, and it felt good to be part of the process in the end. Their struggle, however, could have augured inauspiciously for my solo attempt to move the tree later that day. But Deer Candy had previously reassured me in his nonchalant way that he never had any trouble moving similar two-foot root balls using a tarp to drag it. Though there was a 20-year disparity in age between us, I had told myself that if Deer Candy could do it, I could do it. I had just confirmed that belief when I planted the root ball of the red maple tree a few weeks earlier.

Deer Candy finally showed his respect for the weight of the root ball by using a forklift to manipulate it into the car. Anticipating my job to come, he put a heavy-duty piece of cardboard beneath the root ball that would slide along with it when removing the tree from the back of the van. He and his co-worker then filled the van with the tree so that the upper reaches of the branches projected between the two front captain chairs. They did not damage a twig of the bound branches and left only a smattering of dirt around the root ball. Had you been there, you would not have been happy with the room remaining for you between one of the middle and front captain chairs. As we said our goodbyes and expressed our thanks, Deer Candy's attention was already beginning to turn toward a couple of spry women in their early sixties who were dressed for gardening in flannel and jeans and warming their hands with cups of coffee. I could feel the page was beginning to turn on our interlude of comic relief. Yet, I was thankful to you for bringing about this wonderful episode on a wild and beautiful day that resounded more with life than the passing of it.

****

While putting you in the ground that afternoon, I was the Rabbi, a member of the bereaved family, and the mainstay of the burial crew. Early on, I was most focused on the last responsibility, accomplishing the task efficiently without mishap. I had visions of supporting you awkwardly or dropping you, hearing your ribs crack or your body thud. We had to move your 100 pounds of dead weight from the screened-in back porch to the grave, one hundred feet down the gentle slope of our side yard. I did not want to throw you around and drop you like a sack of potatoes; I still had too much respect for the life inside your corpse. Yet the wheelbarrow seemed like the most appropriate hearse to transport you from the bottom of the porch steps to the hole awaiting you. I slid your bed with you on it across the porch to the swinging screen door. Then Cindy and I lifted you, using the sheet as a stretcher, and carried you down the stairs to the awaiting wheelbarrow. I took most of your weight by reaching for the center of the sheet, all the while sensing Cindy's fear that I would either hurt myself or spill you into the holly bushes on either side of the steps. The wheelbarrow rocked with your weight as you landed slightly askew, but did not tip over. The bed of the wheelbarrow, as old as you were, held all of you but your hind legs which extended stiffly over the edge.

I was heedful of the indignity of hauling you like a big bag of peat moss. So I put the hearse in overdrive and sped you down to your grave. At the gravesite, Cindy did not see the manpower among us to get you into the grave with the grace and dignity required, but she had failed to account for the adrenalin that was coursing through me at that moment. (You never would have known if we had dumped you unceremoniously, but that was not an image with which we wanted to live.) I climbed into the grave and unfurled a deep blue throw rug that usually sat at the doorway to the kitchen and protected the carpet while you lounged there expectantly, monitoring the activity around the refrigerator. Then I asked Cindy to tip the wheelbarrow in my direction toward the grave so that I could ease you down to the rug. Without any perceptible strain, I gave you a forgettable soft landing.

I positioned your body in the grave and prepared to look at you one last time. The grave held you comfortably with an inch or two to spare for your extended hind leg and even more headroom. I crouched beside you and began to run my hand along your torso as my vision blurred with tears. Such a wonderful, naughty, robust, magical dog. I invited Cindy down into your tomb with me to be with you one last time. In climbing down, she kicked some dirt from the edge onto your fur. I yelled, "Don't do that!" My venom took her aback; she apologized. I knew this dirt was but a taste of things to come, but I was not yet ready to allow the earth to lay a finger on you. I wanted to remember your handsome blond, red, and white fur unmarred by death's trappings. Obsessively brushing the dirt from your side, I apologized profusely to Cindy and let her have her goodbyes with you. Together, we wrapped you in our human shield.

Besides the throw rug and your protective sheet, we had gathered several items that had brought you joy in your earthly life to help you make the transition to your new home. The night before, in part out of habit, but mostly to honor you, I did not eat my pizza crust. Besides I had no appetite for it; only later did it occur to me what an appropriate parting gift it would be. We found one of your algae-plastered boulders from Suttons Bay. Cindy brought a four-by-six photo of your human family. I found a half eaten rawhide bone that you had lost the energy to finish. We arranged the boulder and the perishable things around your snout. Oh so lovingly we arranged them. Oh so lovingly. I helped Cindy from the grave and tucked you as airtight as I could in the sheet. And then I went around the sheet one more time to check the seal.

Neither Cindy nor I had prepared any words. We planned a memorial service when the rest of your human family was home. So I do not recall specifically what either of us said as we stood overlooking your wrapped corpse, though I suspect we offered a few words of gratitude and a brief farewell. We had not discussed it beforehand, but it felt natural to fall back on Jewish tradition at this moment. Accordingly, I threw a shovelful of dirt on your shroud and then she did the same. Then, I undid much of the work I had done to make your final home, shoveling, kicking, and pushing the sand back into hole from which it had come, as if doing it quickly put you out of your misery that much sooner. (I know that it was probably my misery to which I was reacting.) When the sand had reached a depth that I was certain would shield you from the impact of my foot, I stepped into the hole and tamped the sand with increasing might to seal you from varmints.

To finish your burial, I had only to plant your dogwood. After we had returned from the nursery, I had backed the van with Cindy's guidance through the yard and around a raised bean-shaped garden to the unobstructed northeastern edge of your grave, leaving enough room to incline a board from the back of the van to the edge of your grave. Once I filled your grave halfway, I measured the depth of the dogwood's root ball and finished filling in your grave to approximate this depth. Then, I used the most handy 6-foot board of one-by-twelve cedar siding from the garage as a narrow and flimsy ramp from the back of the van to the edge of your grave. Fearing that the root ball of the dogwood would snap the cedar board like a twig, I braced it near the center of its descent with concrete blocks. To manipulate the root ball, I wound heavy-duty nylon rope through the weave of the metal basket surrounding it. Cindy thought that the whole operation looked precarious. I don't know that I disagreed with her, but I reassured her anyway and moved ahead without hesitating.

I struggled to budge the root ball over the lip of the back of the van while Cindy stood on the low end of the inclined board to stabilize it. Once the root ball was out of the van on a ramp that was narrower than it was, all it wanted to do, it seemed, was to take a short cut to the ground, off the edge of the ramp. I had to use as much of my energy to prevent the root from moving sideways as I did to move it down the ramp. In the end, the cedar board slipped off the lip of the van but was caught by the concrete blocks just as the root ball slid into the bed of your half-filled grave. The perfect landing provided a brief moment of needed triumph, and I sent my gratitude to the gods that decide which bonehead plans are going to work out on any given day.

I rocked and twisted the root ball in the hole until it was oriented in the most pleasing way to Cindy's eye. Then Cindy held the trunk of the tree while I stabilized the root ball with some of the sandy soil that remained. When the tree was stabilized, I filled in the hole, trying to reconstruct the same layers that I had removed, before blending in the freshly turned soil of the grave with much of the garden behind it. By the time I surrounded the base of the dogwood with wood chips, to the naive eye it would have appeared that a nice dogwood had just been planted in a freshly tilled garden. There was been minimal evidence of the solemn event that had occasioned the tree.

Arm in arm, Cindy and I stood before the freshly planted tree. Already, there were moments when you became the tree, your spirit in it, and nurturing it became the same as nurturing you. There were moments as well when the tree stood only as a sentry over your corpse in your tomb. And there were moments when the tree's only purpose was to collapse you ribcage. During all these moments, you were present as much as you were absent. Your crisis behind us and forever within us had shown us, two humans, the beauty of working harmoniously for something we loved during the most difficult of times. Arm in arm, each of us understood this would be your legacy, not the harassing ways of your youth. We stood before the dogwood and willed your spirit into it.

We cleared the area of the van, wheelbarrow, and garden tools, and set a hose to trickle at the base of your tree, even though I knew that the moisture might invite more rapid decay four feet below. The decay was inevitable, I tried to reason, and the tree would be the reservoir of your spirit for years to come. This would be our first instance of nourishing your memory and visiting you in this tree, and even the thought of providing fluids to the insects and saprophytes that would feast on your remains would not deter a commitment to assiduous care for your tree. Eventually, we were able to withdraw from the solemn ground of the tree. We stood 25 yards away where the yard adjoined the driveway near the basketball pole and looked at the newcomer tree with silvery branches, young and healthy in its near winter nakedness, set apart from a battalion of experienced, native trees behind it. These trees were the citizens of your former haunt. Hopefully, they would accept your immigrant tree as one who had been among them in a previous life. For Cindy and me, looking from this short distance across our yard, the transformation was nearly complete. We accepted this tree as what remained physically of you. We mourned you when we looked at this tree, and, we celebrated you.

****

Mostly, though, I endured the pain of your absence the next few days. At some point, I began to write this remembrance to understand the immense emotion associated with your loss, because I could not contain it within me, and because things had happened that I never wanted to forget. So far, I have captured the beauty and pathos of things that I never wanted to forget. I have expressed enough of my pain in the printed word that it is more tolerable, though certainly time has mercifully provided its balm as well. But at this moment, having wound back to my point of departure, I have barely touched on why your leaving was so painful for me. I still have this feeling, possibly universal among those who experience pain from a loss, that if the pain does not lead to some greater understanding of life and myself, then I will remain scarred, a casualty of the experience, rather than a more complete human being, strengthened and deepened by the experience. You took me to school in a way that few have and I need to understand the point of your lessons.

Had I not cared for you, I would not have been pained by your illness and death. When we love or care about anything, we take a risk nearly proportional to the depth of feelings we have for it. I let you into my being without considering the consequences, I believe, because you were "just a dog." Humans had hurt me before, but I had not considered that a non-human animal could hurt me. So innocently, I allowed you to give me joy and disappointment. I took care of your simple needs, and in return, with unmatched loyalty and consistency (not that it was perfect by any means), without flaunting your good will, you took care of my psyche and erased many of my lonely moments. You accomplished this feat so spontaneously, with so little fanfare, that I had no idea the extent to which your being wove itself into my life. Perhaps, were I more outgoing with dozens of acquaintances and friends, you would not have been able to assume this role in my life. But as I am one of those people who can express his love for humanity by working in a caring profession, without forming many long lasting friendships in my personal life, you fell into this role. At most times, if someone had asked me, I would have said that I found this balance fulfilling. I believe that I generally radiate relatively sound emotional health. So I do not want to cast your role as a fix for a fundamental flaw in myself and others like me. I am merely suggesting that like many others, I may have been more susceptible to the charms of a dog. You earned and deserved my attention, care, and devotion, my love. I willingly took the risk of letting you into my life and heart, and when you left, I, as a human, experienced the pain of your absence. Knowing the outcome, I would do it again and will do it again with one of your brethren.

Many times, when I have shared your loss with other pet owners, they have sympathized with the statement, "A pet is part of the family." At first, the phrase seemed so trite it provided only hollow solace. What exactly did they mean anyway? How could an animal that did not share part of our human gene pool be part of the family? They were not saying that the pet was a favorite uncle or aunt. I believe that they were saying that their pets were an integral part of their nuclear family, the family that made up their everyday home life. They were really trying to say that the relationship with their pet was special enough and unique enough that "family" became the best and most familiar human term to describe it.

So, at the risk of being offensive, I will try to

understand the human-canine relationship and the loss of a dog in "family" terms. But first, I must say that I hope to God that I remain naïve to the experience of losing a child. In addition to the gaping emotional wound it would open, implied in the loss of a child are the endless ruminations about "what might have been", and the loss of a generation. The profound strain of the loss of a child, unlike our loss of you, creates as much potential to erode human relationships as it does to strengthen them. This being said, it is still worthwhile to mention the similarities between an adult human's relationship to a young child and to a dog. Like a young child, a dog is constantly under foot and remains nearly completely dependent on an adult's care. A dog owner, like the parent of the child, is at the center of his dog's universe. He tries to establish routines for his dog to meet not only his nutritional and health needs, but also his emotional needs, canine fun and joy. In the end, an adult trains and instructs both his dog and his children as much as possible to fit into a human community.

But as far as this parallel might go, and I could take it further, there are at least three relevant fundamental differences between a child and a pet. Our goal in raising a child is to make him an independent, functioning member of the human community whereas a dog remains dependent and becomes only more so with aging. When we enter a relationship with a dog, though rarely at the forefront of our thoughts, we anticipate outliving him and one day having to say goodbye to him. Finally, while every dog is unique, we can replace it with another one that will have many of the same behavioral traits, especially if it is of the same breed. These differences mitigate the pain of losing a dog, but also make it inevitable, and, in one respect, makes it more painful, because the dependent bond is as strong as it is with a 3 or 4 year old child. One begins to understand why the eternal absence of a dog might be felt as profoundly, at least for a brief time, as the absence of a young child.

But an aging dog is like another family member as well, an aging parent who has lost his independence. Like an aging parent, an aging dog is sedentary with predictable patterns of responses and whereabouts. He can be sagacious and comforting with few words, just by being present. He requires constant attention to his daily needs, eating, getting around, and elimination. His care can be draining at times, robbing the household of sleep and needed vacations, because of the unpredictability his health. There are times when the caretaker ponders the balance between the misery of a depleted capacity to live and the small pleasures that this diminished capacity still permits. Somehow, life usually tips the scale in its favor. As a dog owner or a child with an aging parent, it is possible to visualize the end, but not possible to know all the ramifications of the final absence. When the end comes, it might be expected, but in spite of all the burdens born until that moment, it is rarely routine or desired.

But there are obvious differences. For our parents, we often harbor ambiguous emotions from a much longer and more complicated history together. Residual anger or resentment from past injuries may keep us away at the end or envelop us with guilt, leaving us with a different kind of terminal torture. Even more obvious, as much as our parent might desire it, while we have the option to withdraw care at the end, we do not have the option to end life at a designated moment; we cannot euthanize our human loved ones. Still the process of caring for and losing an aging, dependent parent shares enough in common with the process of caring for our aging dogs that we feel that they too are family.

Perhaps, the best way to understand why a dog feels like a family member is to consider the sheer magnitude of opportunities we have to form a bond with our dogs. Such a bond could only form within a nuclear family. What is the bond between two living entities but the final outcome of millions of interactions brought about by millions of moments together, many of which are unnoticed or subliminal? Izzy, from the time we got up to the time we went to bed, and at times, even while we slept, you were a constant presence in our lives. Cindy was comforted by your soft snoring rhythm at night when her sleep cycles brought her prematurely to consciousness. When I brushed my teeth in the morning, most mornings, I peered into our bedroom through the bathroom doorway to see if you lay beside the bed waiting for your next opportunity to score a biscuit. Before you lost your hearing and the bounce in your legs, when I arrived home at night, you would charge down the wooden floor of the hallway and slide into me. Come night, you and I would occupy our king size bed like yin and yang, usually with me conforming to the space that you left. In the morning, you subjected me to your piercing eyes, pleading for just one more biscuit before I walked through the mudroom door into the garage. These are just a few of the obvious interactions. It does not take into account the infinite number of moments that passed unnoticed to my consciousness when your snout rested between your front paws, or when you bounced three times to conclude your deer chase through the woods, or when your rock hounding at Sutton's Bay formed the backdrop to my reverie. I could go on endlessly—thousands of glances in your direction, thousands of thoughts about where you might be or what you might be doing when out of sight, thousands of adjustments to your presence. All of these instances went into forming my bond with you. This bond grew and strengthened because of proximity and opportunity, both of which can take place only in a nuclear family. Perhaps we are fortunate that you and your ilk are "only dogs" because if you were human, we would never bond with another like you to avoid the pain that comes at the end.

After you died, I had difficulty confessing how much more I was broken up by your death than my father's nine months earlier. I loved my father, and if I could magically bring one of you back right now, I hope you would understand that it would be my father. No one will ever fill the shoes of my father, but another dog will probably fill most of the void that you left behind. I believe that this paradox is best explained by the difference in the day-to-day roles that each of you played in my life. For thirteen years, I had spent a good portion of every day with you, and this only intensified at the end. My father lived three hundred miles away in my hometown, Cincinnati, and entered my life mainly through phone calls that occurred regularly once or twice a week. These were usually marathon phone calls that we both had a hard time closing because of our mutual respect and love for each other. He cared and asked about the most important elements of my life, more than anyone else on the face of the earth. His care was not adulterated by the usual self-interest that others have, as long as I gave him my respect, which in the final decades, I gave easily. My visits and phone calls only intensified at the end. But my father had done his job as a parent in the end, that is, making sure that I could function in a complicated, frequently unkind world without his physical presence.

Izzy, your presence, on the other hand, had become very much part of my daily and indeed, moment-to-moment, emotional well-being. You expressed the joy and innocence of a young child who worshipped his parents like a god until the end. You were the undemanding aged loved one who got what he gave at the end of his life. You were woven into my life and heart, responding to who I was unconditionally. My father, on the other hand, was much of who I am, and I necessarily carry him inside wherever I go. I miss him, but all I need do is look inside. I miss you and I look to a dogwood to remind me of the joy and still the pain.

Izzy, your life's lessons do not end just yet. My experience at the end with you allowed me to understand the relationship between elderly spouses. I must confess that I did not understand how elderly spouses seemed to love each other so deeply when each of them was a ghost of what they had been formerly. I even considered their attachment, somewhat cynically, a pathologic dependence. At some point, I started asking my elderly lovebird patients to bring a wedding picture to their appointments, believing that seeing an image of their youthful relationship was the key to understanding their love in their gray, wizened, visually impaired, hard-of-hearing state.

One lovebird in his ninth decade was so grateful to me for providing what he believed was lifesaving care to his beloved wife in the hospital that he designed and built a cherry stepstool so that I could reach the books on the upper shelves of the cherry bookcases in my study. Another woman, in spite of constant back pain that shot down to both feet, spent an hour every morning dressing her husband's swollen red toes that were starved for blood and remained viable only because of her tender loving care. He was kind, good natured, and non-complaining, but incapable of forming new memories; yet she clearly dreaded the moment when a minor ill wind would extinguish the last little flame of his life.

On the whole, even if I did not completely understand it, I began to admire the chemistry that created the blaze between these lovebirds, even when one or both of their flames flickered. Now, I not only admire it, I believe that I understand the bond, a bond that developed over the decades of caring about each other, that was amplified rather than diminished in their graying, golden years. Izzy, my love for you has taught me a great deal about aging and about people aging together, leaving me hopeful that I will someday tend this enduring flame with Cindy, even as our individual ones subside to embers. Izzy, it is said by those who wish to emasculate the power of death and dying that we are dying from day we are born. While this may hold some truth, there is clearly a time when our star seems to be rising, and another when it seems to be falling. We anticipate and celebrate the former and dread and condescend to the latter. You have taught me that beauty and wisdom exists even as our stars approach the western horizon. Cindy and I immersed ourselves in your far western journey and watched the heavens explode with streaks and striations of crimson, pink and iridescent orange in heavens of surrealistic blue. Your dying engendered an intensity of living rarely matched in our tending to the rising stars in our life. Our love for you will live on in our love for each other. In the end, that is your unique gift.

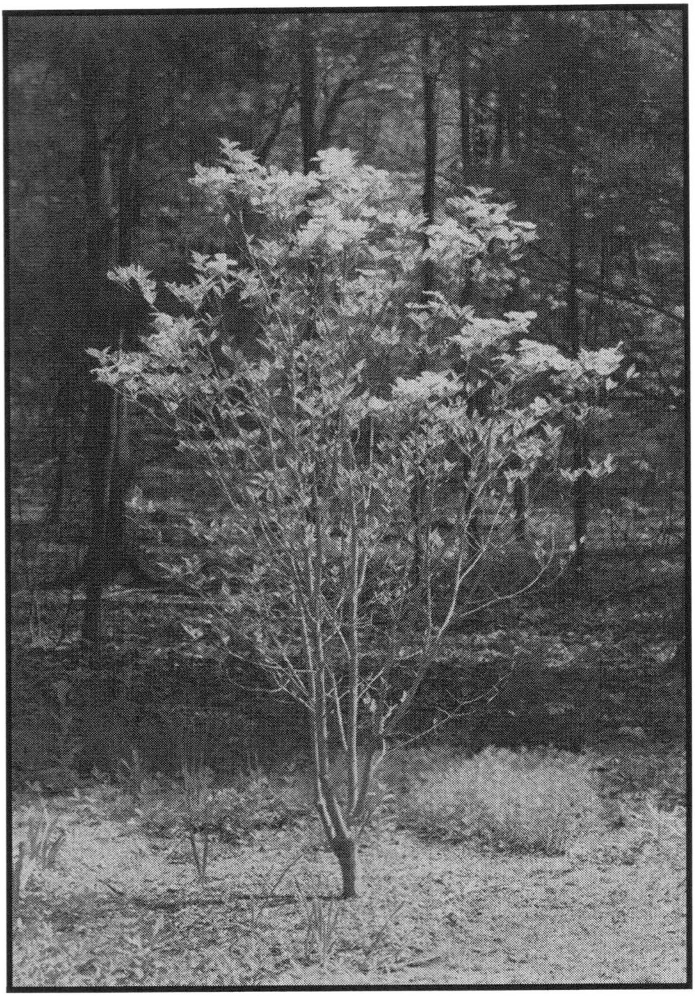

Epilogue

    I did not write the preceding pages to bring you back to life; that would be magical thinking. No, I wrote them to keep you alive. Yet, when l look at your pictures placed in view in most rooms within our house, I notice that the pain of letting you go is beginning to remit, and that no matter how hard I concentrate, I am having trouble remembering your particular smell, your particular blend of red, white, and blond fur, and your particular way of responding to me, all those things that for years, I took for granted, that I now wish I had encapsulated in an airtight chamber in my cerebrum. I must admit that a chocolate Labrador retriever has come between me and my memories of you. For months he has created and occupied a space between Cindy and me in bed at night, the same space that you once created and that aging took from you. His name is Jesse and his behavior cannot help but invite comparisons to yours.

    Jesse has been with us now for four months, and as of today, he is two years old. Cindy was the first who could not bear the solitude that your absence created in the house when she returns home in the late afternoon to a large empty house after a school day of teaching. I have always had the luxury of returning home from work to Cindy. At the time she started looking in the classified for another dog, I was still entrenched in my grieving and was not quite ready to "replace you." However, once I realized that Cindy planned to bring another life into our house, I became involved in weighing the different options available on the Internet classified.

Before we found Jesse, we had already e-mailed someone who raises Labs in a neighboring state. But when we found Jesse's listing, it seemed almost too good to be true—an AKC chocolate lab, year and a half old, looking for a loving household, $300. We both found the trade-off acceptable--we might face his death after a shorter period, 11 or 12 years, if he lived as long as you, but we would not have to lose sleep house-breaking him. All he had to have was some of your vitality and most of your good looks. When we went to meet him several days later in Rockford, Michigan, a fun loving, sleek, handsome brown dog greeted us by jumping on the screen door well before we saw a human face. At that instant, we knew we would be driving home with him.

Jesse does not have your girth, your wayward blond-red hair, your penchant for boulders, your deep ferocious bark, your obsession with food, and your general alpha-male canine machismo. He is a gentle, loving 75-pound lapdog. Rather than harassing our neighbors with an unfriendly volley of barking and forays meant to chase them to the next county, he invites himself into their cars when they open the car door to exit. He shows the same intensity for tennis balls that you did for food and rocks. He has littered our yard with tennis balls in much the same way you littered the Suttons Bay back yard with Traverse Bay boulders. In the same way that your day revolved around your next opportunity to receive food, Jesse's day revolves around his next opportunity to chase and chew a tennis ball. Before you left us, you met my younger son's girlfriend, and greeted her with a few off-putting nips at her hand and a low-pitched growl. Even in your mellowed, mostly deaf, aged state, you managed to make a card-carrying dog lover wary of your presence. With Jesse, she fell in love at first sight. When she comes to visit, she looks forward to seeing him at least as much as she does to seeing us, and when we travel in the van together, she welcomes Jesse to melt in her lap. Jesse is milk chocolate and a spring shower; you were an acquired cruciferous taste and a cold morning swim.

We had not had Jesse for more than two weeks when I experienced an inkling of the canine change of guard in our household. I wrote about it in my journal. "Is it reasonable to allow a dog to define the eras in our household? If so, we have entered a new one in the last two weeks, grieving the end of the Izzy era and welcoming in the Jesse era. Today, walking home from Deerlick along the creek, we were awed by Jesse's unrestrained, canine athleticism and joy. For the entire 15-minute hike, he raced, bounded, and leaped, at times charging down the sheer vertical wall into the creek and bounding up its basketball player height as if gravity lost its hold. The surrounding forest, laced with briars and criss-crossed by downed trees, dense with brush and booby trapped with vines, he navigated full-throttle, no hesitation and not a hitch. He sliced and turned and veered and leaped, and at one point, in the process of making a 180 turn, just for the fun of it, chased his tail for a couple of 360's before racing back the other direction. He would race just so far ahead of us before he charged back to his new parents, infecting us with a mixture of the joy of parents watching a wide-eyed and open-mouthed toddler discover toddling and the joy of fans watching the superhuman graceful maneuvers of Michael Jordan or Barry Sanders. We experienced a transcendent moment, as the only spectators of this Olympian performance by a beast in which many of the God-given canine talents converged in this one powerful and free-spirited animal." The next day, we returned from the Deerlick Lake Michigan access using the same path in the hope of experiencing the same performance. However, Jesse was not inspired by the same spirit. He was mortal after all. Besides, one cannot plan on being amazed—that must occur spontaneously and unexpectedly.

You need not be concerned that we forgot about you as soon as Jesse re-introduced canine joy into our lives. We only assumed that your youth had occurred too long ago to remember whether you had performed similar feats of canine athleticism. In fact, with Cindy's silent consent, I set out introducing a bit of your naughtiness and feistiness into Jesse. When he came to us, he showed very little interest in food, in general, and gave even less thought to human food. I wished to carry on the tradition that part of any good companionship, even human-canine companionship, is sharing something you have that the other wants. We started offering morsels of pizza crust and the residue of our dinner bowls and plates. Though he has yet to show the zest that you did in snapping up pizza crust, inhaling them in one bite, he now awaits his crust with a streamer of drool coursing from the corner of his mouth. He awaits our plates and bowls quietly (none of your insistent barking) with the same Pavlovian salivation, though his job of dishwashing does not approach yours. He seems to like all the fruits and nuts that I eat, especially apples, bananas, apricots, and cashews, and he does not mind Terra chips. He is, in some ways, a less picky eater than you were; you could have done without apples.

I have also had to teach him to play-wrestle. If ever I lay beside you, you would instantly start mouthing me or jumping on me; this was fun, up to a point, especially once your teeth wore down. Jesse's first move was to roll on his back, showing me his underside, in a submissive pose. He had so little of the alpha male in him that he even urinated like a female rather than contorting his body at every pole and fire hydrant in an effort to shoot urine higher than the rest of the neighborhood dogs. I was not willing to teach him to urinate, but he is beginning to play on his side and show me the inside of his mouth. Still, whereas you always wanted to play, he usually wants to make love by offering his lethargic peaceful affection.

Jesse may strike you as being incorruptible and angelic, but I did not have teach him to terrorize our cats, grab and consume entire loaves of bread from the kitchen counter, hump and bite his brand new bed instead of sleeping on it, and walk around with this squealing whine whenever he is impatient to play tennis ball outside. So you need not worry about going down in the Liscow annals as the Lucifer dog banished by a future chorus of heavenly dogs. You may have inflicted a bruise or a scratch in your lifetime, but you never harmed anyone in any significant way. You were a wonderful home companion, especially after the children left for the next segments of their lives. You were a joy-giving, living fixture in our home and you gave more to its humanity than you demanded from it. You have a successor, who has the potential to fill your paws, and your successor will more than likely have his successor; that is all. You will all be inscribed in bold type as a footnote in the "Book of Life".

So here we go again, opening our hearts to and molding another canine member of our family. Unlike a child, we are not raising him to strike out independently some day and leave us. Yet leave us, he will. We easily recognize the dependence that he has upon us, for food, elimination, play, and training. But in our human chauvinism, we lose sight of the dependence we have upon these creatures who become wonderful human companions without the greatest of human qualities, reason and self-knowledge, lacking the capacity to lead nations and create great works of art. We accept and mold these canine beings who we will someday dearly miss and grieve. We accept this responsibility even though no one yet has conceived of a god that helps us mourn our dogs; we make such a firm line between human life and all other life. I suppose we leave it to the canine kingdom to help us mourn the loss of our dogs. Izzy, as painful as it was to lose you, you left behind enough joy and beauty, that someday, I will once again immerse myself in one of love's final journeys, the care of another dying dog.

A FATHERS LAST HOURS THROUGH THE EYES OF HIS PHYSICIAN SON

My father's last day, I must confess with some unease, was an extraordinary day for me. I experienced it on multiple levels assuming multiple roles, interwoven at times and distinct at others. At times, I was the physician in charge, making diagnostic assessments, deciding upon general care, and explaining the illness and its progression to the family, my family. Other times, as the one with the least inexperience, I assumed the role of nurse, administering rectal medications and disintegrating oral medications. Unusual for a physician, I had the opportunity to observe first-hand the minute-by-minute progression of the terminal portion of a terminal illness; we usually try to maintain an objective distance. Without my usual distance and relative equanimity, the assessments of my father's condition and their associated expectations changed maddeningly from hour to hour during the first half of the day, the period of greatest diagnostic uncertainty. Not only was I guiding my family through the last day, but I was also guiding myself—as a physician, I may have found this path somewhat familiar, but as the son, I was in new emotional territory. Naturally, I agonized over my assessments and decisions because I was making them for my father. Most of the day, I knew that the sudden change in his condition signaled the end, but I never thought until his last breath that the end would occur that day. I had not hesitated to doctor my father because, fundamentally, I knew that he would have wanted it that way. Caring for him with his tacit approval was a profound privilege. Nevertheless, I experienced the day mainly as a concerned, struggling, grieving son.

 The night before his final day, my father's weakness from years of fighting prostate cancer reached a new depth. Throughout it all, he had maintained his memory for business associates, hardware, and all the minute daily details of his many medications like a thirty year old, his way of maintaining some control while the illness sapped him physically. Yet he had lost his stamina to focus on sustained conversation and he communicated in short phrases before wearing himself out. He was taking his meager meals in bed by then, but his dignity still found the strength to make the 20-foot trip with one right turn and two left turns to his raised toilet into what had become his dedicated bathroom. That night, in his king-sized bed in his TV-lit room, we both took turns dozing off while watching the depleted Cincinnati Bearcat basketball team lose to Syracuse in a blowout. Until then, my father had been passionate enough about University of Cincinnati Basketball that it was hard for him to watch the close games (he was either riveted to the TV or turning away in anguish). He not only watched no more than a play or two, but at times, he forgot that the game was on. Between naps, his voice trailed off when asking about it, and a few times, he asked the same question later. Since the game had been a blowout, I blamed the Cincinnati performance for part of my father's malaise; they should have given a dying man a better game to watch. I too should have given him a better performance with more enthusiasm and less dozing; knowing it was among my last evenings with him, I should not have left him that night so unfulfilled.

I slept that night in the downstairs guest room with a new premonition that his bathroom trips in the middle of the night posed a danger to him. That must be why I heard every thump of my mother's racing steps down the hallway from her bedroom to my father's room on the opposite side of the house. When the steps stopped, I heard my mother scream. I jumped out of the bed as soon as I heard the steps and felt around in the dark for my sweatpants. I needed to go upstairs at least partially dressed, because I knew what I had just heard, at best, was a broken bone and I had to prepare for an extended period of help. By the time my mother was yelling for me by name, I was cursing under my breath about the whereabouts of my sweatpants. My vehement cursing had its intended effect—it awakened my wife and she found my sweatpants. Then, I raced upstairs.

My mother stood over my father who lay on his left side on the carpet between his bed and the dresser a little more than a body width's away. His head rested on a rust-colored folded body pillow between the door and the foot of his bed, and the rest of his body stretched across the carpet toward the head of the bed. He did not look uncomfortable or obviously injured, and he could give us no indication of how long he had been resting there. He was awake and seemed to recognize me as his son and as someone who might help him get back into bed. At that point, my mother and I assumed that he had fallen, either going to or coming back from the bathroom.

His mouth was dry and nearly immovable. He spoke unclearly with hardly any stamina, as if his narcotics, sleep deprivation, and his cancer had combined to drain it completely from him. He was able to put a Vicodin in his mouth and swallow it in preparation for the pain that might be associated with moving him from the floor back to the bed. He wanted in the worst way to accomplish this maneuver himself, leaving little doubt about his ability to form an intention. With minimal assistance from me, he sat up on the floor, and he continued to show great interest in getting into bed. He did not seem to understand, however, that he needed to straighten his right leg that remained curled beneath him. He remained alert and implored me as much with his eyes as his short phrases to get him into bed. I crouched in front of him without a clear plan, knowing only that his dignity required me to end this helpless situation and that I needed a miracle to get him on his feet.

I asked him to put his arms around my neck to minimize the pressure I would have to use reaching below his armpits for his cancer-riddled shoulder blades. He was able to weakly clasp his hands around my neck, but I could not lift him without putting a painful amount of pressure on his upper back. After trying it this way a couple of times, I moved behind him to lift him from the rear. Though I did not succeed in budging him an inch from the floor, when I stopped to rethink things, I found that the upper half of my t-shirt was already damp with sweat. I realized what I already suspected at some level, that I was not going to be able to get my dad back in the bed by myself.

My mother, by this time, had mentioned her concern that he might be having a problem similar to one he had had several weeks earlier when he ended up on the floor. During that episode, he had felt like he was walking on a pillow, an event with which my mom was entirely familiar as she had had a similar event called a TIA, an episode in which part of her brain was temporarily deprived of blood and oxygen. Perhaps, he was having a similar episode this time. Whether I verbally or mentally dismissed her idea, I believed that there was enough going on with his cancer to explain everything we were seeing, especially in view of his accelerating weakness and his recent decision to take his meals in bed instead of going to the kitchen. Still, this alternative explanation for my dad's weakness and disorientation had been raised early on in what was going to be his final day.

My mother also considered calling 911, but we both thought better of it because we did not want to transport my father to the hospital and spend any of his remaining days or hours mired in an extended evaluation in the emergency room and hospital. Besides, I thought, if it was manpower we needed, I could call my younger brother by two years to help. But I did not think that we needed to disturb him in the middle of the night yet. There were a couple of egg crate mattresses in the basement, which we could use to make a comfortable bed on the floor. My father could spend the night on the floor until the sun rose and my brother had a full night's sleep. I ran downstairs to our bedroom, grabbed the egg crate mattress and a comforter, giving my wife an update on my dad's status as I did, and then raced upstairs. Laying them toward the doorway, I arranged the two egg crate mattresses and comforter into a comfortable bed behind my seated father. However, even after I coaxed him to lie down, only his head and the upper half of his torso were on the makeshift bed.

I saw no obvious way to move the rest of him that lay helplessly where it had been since he had fallen. I could not pull him by his fragile shoulders, the source of his greatest pain since we had learned that his cancer had spread throughout his bones; something would surely crack. Even though his weight had fallen twenty pounds and counting below his 200-pound weight before his illness, I could not cradle him in my arms like a baby. I did not want my seventy-five year old mother to hurt herself by maneuvering half of his weight. We finally decided to put a bed sheet beneath him and move him in the same way nurses move hospital patients. My mother brought me a sheet, but I still could not roll my father's dead weight and brittle bones. Even if we did manage this, how could I move my dad without creating an impossible role for my mother?

It was time to call my brother. Again, we rejected calling 911. Though hospice had been involved with my father for months, we postponed that call as well until later. My brother's wife answered the phone when I finally called. He said that he would be right over, and in ten minutes, he arrived.

By the time he arrived, my father no longer was satisfied with lying down and wanted to try and get into bed again. He pulled himself up, as desperate as he was determined, and rested his left shoulder against the dresser and his left hand on the floor. He begged me to help, addressing me by name, formulating sentences that were comprehensible overall but garbled in the middle. My assessment of the problem at the moment was unchanged. I reasoned, "Who could make a full sentence with a mouth so dry and a mind fogged in by sleep deprivation and legions of cancer cells?" I did not have to introduce a new diagnosis.

At first, my brother and I deferred to the wishes of my father, who still clung desperately to an upright seated position, and tried to stand him up by allowing him to use one of us as a grab bar. When this maneuver was again unsuccessful, each of us took an arm and reached around to a shoulder blade and tried to lift him unsuccessfully; then one of us tried to lift him from the rear while the other functioned in front as a grab bar, again without success. My dad just did not seem to have the strength, even less than what he had in his extremely weakened state the evening before.

So, my brother and I tried to convince him to lie down so that we could maneuver him onto the orange, thickly padded comforter and use it as a stretcher to lift him into bed. But he either did not understand why we wanted him to lie down or he could not hear us; perhaps, he just wanted to do it his own way. Who knew at the time? All reasons were plausible. After ignoring my brother and me multiple times, he finally responded to my firm command and a thorough explanation of why he needed to lie down. I had never before used that tone of voice with my father, but we were running out of options. I had abandoned my pleading son's voice and found my rarely used commanding doctor's voice.

Already, I had created more room to maneuver my dad by moving the bed and nightstand on the opposite side of the bed toward the opposite wall. My brother and I together were able to pull the draw sheet beneath my dad, and with surprising ease, dragged him to the middle of the comforter. Then, using the makeshift bed as a stretcher, we lifted him into bed, placing him with his head at the foot of the bed and his feet at the head. There he lay peacefully until he seemed to recognize that his world had rotated 180 degrees; using the quilt as a draw sheet, we rotated him into his familiar orientation and centered him safely in the bed.

****

Shortly after he was situated, he sat up on the usual side

of the bed near his big dresser that held, among other things, all his medications. He was fidgety and was oddly wide-eyed. Fearing that all the moving had reignited his pain, we offered him another Vicodin. He seemed to want it, but rather than opening his mouth to receive it, I had to shove it between his lips. I brought a glass of water to his lips and he admitted the straw to his mouth. I watched the level of water in the glass, willing it to drop while exhorting him to drink. The few drops that he managed to suck from the glass ran from his mouth. I tried to retrieve the Vicodin tablet with a sweep of my finger before he choked on it, but I did not find it in his mouth or in the runoff. We all squirmed, imagining the bitter taste of the tablet, but hoped that it would bring the same relief as a swallowed tablet.

Habit tried to take over for a time. For months, my father had sat on the edge of his bed for hours at a time to alleviate the discomfort of lying on one of his beleaguered shoulders. He made this move by grabbing a folded walker wedged between the bed and the nightstand, first pulling himself to his side and then pushing himself up. Sometimes, he would head off to the bathroom or to the kitchen for one of his mealets. But more often than not, he needed a different set of pressure points and would remain sitting. If no one was in the room, or if he was too drained to converse, he usually looked for or asked for his electronic Yatzi game. This morning, he sought the same positions, but at an accelerated pace. No sooner was he comfortable lying down, he would roll over to sit again. Since we had removed the walker when moving the bed, my brother and I were forced to assist this frenzied behavior to prevent an injury. He also seemed to lose his preference for the side of the bed facing the doorway and the activity of the house, and began to roll toward the other side. He made these moves with a determined stubbornness that was familiar to my brother and me, leaving us no choice but to follow his lead.

In contrast to his behavior, his speech was becoming progressively less comprehensible, strewn with non-sensible syllables frequently enough that we were beginning to worry that he had lost all clarity of thinking. I asked him if he wanted his Yatzi, mainly to determine if he knew what to do with it. He seemed to understand the question and indicated with a hand gesture that he wanted it. When I gave it to him, he cradled it in his hand and looked at it with a gust of recognition, and it seemed that any moment he would commence to push the button that rolled the electronic dice. But as time passed and he failed to push the button, the look evolved from one of recognition to one of innocent curiosity, and finally to one of complete loss of interest. In the end, he did not seem to know what to do with it and it remained cupped in his right hand; he never would push the roll button again. Ignoring the Yatzi game in his right hand that for weeks had been his lifeline was consequential and ominous to all of us.

****

Later, my mother tried to recall the last comprehensible phrases my dad uttered before he deteriorated into complete gibberish and then into silence. My older sister did as well, as if these words somehow had the same import as other once-in-a-lifetime events, such as seeing Haley's comet or the Northern lights in Cincinnati; though she had arrived well into the transition of his loss of language, she recalled that he said "something" she understood shortly after she arrived. Before she arrived, however, I had already assessed his ability to use and understand words. As he had done reflexively for months, when asked how he was doing or if he was experiencing any pain, he said, "I'm OK." One time, when asked how he was doing, he said, "I'm better." Usually, encouraged by these comprehensible phases, I would try to follow it with a more complex question like, "Do you want your hardboiled egg with mayonnaise," or simply, "Are you hungry. Do you want something to eat?" He never responded to these questions with words, eye movement, or body language that suggested comprehension.

    Only my brother claims to have heard the three most important words my father spoke before his speech was completely erased. One of the times after my dad went from sitting to lying, he experienced a spell that alarmed me enough that I thought the end could be close, possibly imminent. My father's eyes during the ordeal that morning had remained open to a variable extent in their natural state, the left one more than the right due to a partially paralyzing injury to his right facial nerve in the Korean War. After lying down this time, my mother flanked him on the right side and tried to comfort him. Instead of gazing in the direction of her soothing words, he looked toward me on the opposite side where I remained after helping him lie down. The innocence of incomprehension suddenly departed from his eyes. They opened wide, terrified, staring at the ceiling as if looking upon the glowing orbs of a snarling Cerberus at the gates of hell. His jaw clenched down hard and his breath began to make a moist hissing sound as it eked through the paralyzed opening of the right side of his mouth. An ashen color spread rapidly from the bearded area around his mouth and nose, enveloping his entire face, before draining completely to a deathly paleness as his breathing slowed and became barely perceptible. Not knowing what the end would look like, alarmed that the Vicodin from 10 or twenty minutes earlier might have lodged in his vocal cords and cut off his breathing, I panicked and determined that it was time to call my older sister; I knew that the tinderbox of her love and fear had the potential to magnify my 3 alarm concern to an uncontrolled wildfire, but she needed to know about her beloved father, before his last breath.

At this critical moment, the hospice nurse returned a call we had placed earlier, rescuing me from the peril of the unknown, and we arranged an emergency visit within the next hour. Then, I left the room to make the call to my older sister. By the time I returned, my father lay there more relaxed breathing steadily with the color of life. As he emerged from this spell, my brother took the helm beside my dad and he watched him turn to my mother, who was now to his left which his gaze now favored. He watched my father reach up to hug her and say, "I love you." My mom, who had not had a moment to put in her hearing aids, never heard the words, but by the day's end, the departing sentiment was embedded in the lore of the day.

When I called my older sister's house around seven in the morning, about two and a half hours after my mom found my father resting on the floor, her husband answered the phone and then gave it to my sister. I did not finish my first sentence without choking back my tears. My sister, already alarmed by the early morning call, read my faltering voice loud and clear, and started wailing uncontrollably on the other end of the phone. I tried to tell her simply that dad did not seem to be doing very well and I thought that she should come over. Eventually, her husband must have taken back the phone and I briefly explained the events of the morning.

By the time my older sister arrived in my father's sick room, he was again sitting on the usual side of the bed. She immediately walked up to him and knelt with her head bowed so that he might stroke her baby smooth bald head, a side-effect of her own encounter with cancer, breast cancer. For weeks, both my dad and sister took pleasure in this ritual, my sister enjoying the cool hands on her pate overheated by her wig and my father enjoying the soft stubble on adult-sized head of his grown baby daughter. To my sister's disappointment, my father did not take his cue. She raised her head to explain what she was doing and cajoled him to rub her head. Only after the third request, and with a little help that I did not see, did he finally rest his hand on top of her head. She was gleeful with this good sign.

Again we tried to elicit some comprehensible words from him. When asked how he was doing, he might have said that he was "OK" but he said little else, and specifically, did not seem to understand any further questions about breakfast. He also was having more trouble than ever managing his saliva and we found ourselves using Kleenex to prevent his t-shirt from getting soaked. As had been his custom in his final weeks, he favored sitting up with his head bowed, as if sleeping upright or looking down at his Yatzi game.

When he did lay down, my sister cuddled and stroked him on one side and my mom snuggled on the other. My mother's face was more careworn than I had ever seen it, her brown eyes black and bottomless, every worry line etched deeper, and her hair awry from distraught hands pushing through it.

I went downstairs to get my wife because I believed my father's situation was dire. I told her, "I think you better come upstairs now. I think my father is dying."

****

By the time the Hospice nurse arrived for her emergency visit, my sister-in-law had arrived and my wife was upstairs.

Both took part in the family conference. Up until the Hospice nurse arrived, I had struggled with some diagnostic uncertainty about what was causing my father's change in behavior and weakness. Applying a cardinal rule in medicine, I tried to explain all his symptoms using the one illness that I knew about, and tried not to introduce a new diagnosis, even when it seemed it might do a better job of explaining his symptoms. The prostate cancer had massively invaded many of my father's bones including multiple ribs, his pelvis, his shoulder blades, his skull, and his spine, consuming a significant amount of my father's nutritional intake, while at the same time severely inhibiting my father's appetite. Weeks earlier, his lab tests had already shown a moderate drop in his red blood cells and a major drop in his albumin, the protein that was a good gauge of his nutritional status, and both had probably only deteriorated in the intervening weeks. My father's fluid intake had been marginal for weeks, making it likely that dehydration was causing problem for his kidneys.

There were no obvious localizing neurologic symptoms such as a weak arm or a weak leg, only extreme generalized weakness and a very dry mouth, so I assumed that he was unable to talk and maneuver himself because of severe weakness, dehydration, renal failure, low blood pressure with poor blood flow to the brain, and the sedating effect of the narcotics required to control his pain. Even when his mental abilities deteriorated further, I thought that it might have been related to kidney failure and poor blood flow to his brain; his gray color and intermittent spells of sweating, consistent with low blood pressure, seemed to confirm this opinion.

The visiting nurse supplied a single piece of objective information about his blood pressure to derail this line of thought. In an instant I recognized that the most likely explanation for my dad's sudden demise was a stroke. His blood pressure was normal. He had adequate blood flow to the brain, and most likely, to the kidneys as well, making kidney failure less likely. He had no symptoms involving a specific area of his body, but he did have a severely reduced level of consciousness, eye gaze deviation, and difficulties understanding and articulating speech. My new working diagnosis was a stroke involving the blood circulation to the lower centers of the brain, specifically the brainstem, which controlled his level of consciousness, breathing, and other vital functions of the body; to my mind, it was the worst kind of stroke.

I also learned something new from the Hospice nurse about giving medications. She told me that any medication that could be given orally could also be given rectally. She suggested, and I agreed, that we should give my father only medications necessary for his comfort. We pared his medications to Oxycontin, a potent narcotic pain reliever, both to control his pain and to prevent the agitation that might accompany narcotic withdrawal, and to Prednisone, a medication used to decrease inflammation, so that he did not experience withdrawal from it. She suggested that we grind the Vicodin tablets into a paste and place it between his tongue and his cheek where it would be absorbed as well as it would have been from his stomach or his rectum. I figured that I could deliver the Ativan by the same route, a Valium-like medication that we might require to relieve his agitation at some point.

We also had to decide whether to care for my dad at home, or to send him to an inpatient Hospice unit where he could be stabilized. At this point, we did not know exactly how long he was going to live, but we knew that he would require attention around the clock. It seemed clear, however, that he could not live longer than a few days if he was unable to eat or drink, given the weeks of cancer-driven starvation that preceded this final event. None of us really wanted to go to the trouble to transport him to the Hospice center and most of us believed that my father would have preferred to remain at home with his family out of view of friends and strangers alike. I also believed that we would learn more about my father's needs as the day and his illness progressed. We discussed hospital beds and Foley catheters, whether the use of either one of them would make it easier for us to care for my father. We based both of our decisions upon what my father would have wanted, and therefore, decided against the immediate use of the hospital bed available on the other side of the house, and decided to delay the catheter and use an adult diaper instead. Now that we were leaning toward keeping him at home for the duration, we made a list of helpful items. My sister-in-law, who had acquired an excellent set of organizational skills in human resources at General Electric, kept a detailed list of all these items, a list that included, among other things, adult diapers, oral care swabs, absorbent pads, and a draw sheet.

The Hospice nurse was seasoned beyond her thirty-something years, and impressed us with her kindness, calmness, patience, knowledge, and confidence. Her flexibility gave us comfort with any course of action upon which we decided. She recognized the critical nature of my father's change in condition and recommended a daily shift of Hospice nursing that was available on a first come, first serve basis and was based upon the patient's need for it. My father's condition moved him toward the top of the list, but availability was another issue.

After the Hospice nurse left, my sister-in-law, while sitting at the kitchen table, raised the issue of whether my father agreed to an advanced directive of "Do Not Resuscitate." She recalled that my father, when he originally accepted Hospice, did so without truly understanding that he had agreed to "no resuscitation." When it came up again, he was not so sure, and wished to think about it; if he decided he was going to change his directive, he was going to get back with the Hospice nurse. As far as she knew, he never did get back to the Hospice nurse. Nevertheless, my dad had resurrected the issue and raised some doubt, and my sister-in-law felt that it was important at this critical point to voice his doubt. She brought up my father's father who lived over a year after his massive stroke. I distinguished my father's condition from my grandfather's—my father had end stage prostate cancer in addition to the stroke, and even without the stroke, he might not have had more than a couple weeks to live anyway. While I was careful not to be totally dismissive, my father's doubts weeks earlier did not seem relevant at the time. While an important digression, the answer was not complicated under the circumstances and there was no reason to pursue it any further, though she would bring it up briefly again later just to make sure that the issue had sufficient airing.

During the period that followed the departure of the Hospice nurse, I believed that my father suffered from a brainstem stroke, and from the profound weakness of the last stage of prostate cancer. Most of my diagnostic ruminations were tainted with enough doubt that I kept most of them to myself, but when I suggested this possibility out loud, my sister responded, "Those are bad." Enough uncertainty remained in my own mind, however, that subsequent events would change my working diagnoses, more than once.

My father went on to have another spell when his eyes stared wide open, his face tensed in an angry grimace, and his breathing slowed almost to a standstill, but this time I recognized the event as a seizure. The probability that my dad was having recurrent seizures and the probability that I had not recognized several previous ones, opened up another set of diagnostic possibilities associated with different short-term outlooks. It was now possible that much of my dad's change in mental status, possibly even the deterioration in his speech, could be explained as a post-ictal event, changes that occur in the brain in the wake of the massive electrical discharges of a seizure when the brain is trying to restore a functional neurochemical balance. Most likely, I thought that a stroke had injured some brain cells and caused a zone of instability that led to seizures, but I had to consider the possibility that my father's prostate cancer traveled, or metastasized, to the brain and caused the injury that led to the seizures. I Googled the latter possibility and learned that late in the progression of prostate cancer, brain metastases can occur, but rarely.

During this brief period in the evolution in my thinking, I shared these "more sanguine" possibilities with everyone, hypothesizing that if we were able to control the seizures and allow my father to progress through the post-ictal period, he might regain consciousness, become more alert, and possibly speak coherently to us. To this end, after I inserted the Oxycontin and Prednisone, I inserted some Ativan from the Hospice emergency kit, a medication for anxiety, which is also used in emergent situations to control seizures. I subsequently discussed my ruminations and treatment plan with a physician assistant who made home visits and took over my father's care after he became too ill to leave the house. He made a favorable enough impression that my father, on his recommendation, finally agreed to take the anti-depressant, Lexapro, the same medication that I had prescribed for him over a month earlier, but could never convince him to take.

The physician assistant also recommended that we start my father on Dilantin, a common anti-seizure medication, to prevent further seizures. He disagreed with my notion to give high dose Prednisone to reduce any swelling that might be associated with a metastasis to the brain. He did not think that it was worth treating "a hunch." To some extent, I was relieved and grateful to get someone else's informed input, even if it did not completely concur with my own. He also said that I could use up to 2 mg of Ativan if he seized again. Though he knew that I was a doctor, he called in the Dilantin to the Walgreen located in the strip mall down the street from us.

Unfortunately, this Walgreen did not have the requested dose in a tablet form, so we had to settle for large chewable tabs that contained mainly inert ingredients to make it palatable to children; these large tablets only had one-sixth the dose that my father required. Later, I had the unpleasant task of inserting three of these tablets rectally. Though I planned to insert the others hours later when I was sure that the first three dissolved, events mercifully transpired that made this unnecessary.

****

Later, my father's condition evolved in such a way that it clarified for me what the underlying cause was for his change in level of consciousness and his seizures. Though in most ways I was my father's treating physician the day he died, as his son, I was hesitant to treat him like a patient. My examinations tended more toward cursory than thorough. So while he may have had detectable right sided weakness if I had done a more thorough exam early on in the day's events, to the informed eyes of a son, he had no localizing weakness. However, by noon, many hours after my mom's urgent summons to his room, these same eyes noticed that my father was regularly bringing his left hand to his face and forehead while his right arm lay wedged against his body, immobile and limp, like the proverbial dead fish. At first, I may have ignored it, because I had it fixed in my mind that there was no obvious limb weakness. But the activity in his left arm continued while none came from his right. I then noticed that his left leg was flexed at the knee while the right lay still straight out. I performed some very basic comparison tests of the sides of his body, watching him withdraw his left leg to a noxious stimulus, but only moving his foot in response to the same stimulus on the right. I lifted the left hand and forearm off the bed and watched it fall limply without any resistance to the sheets. However, when I did the same maneuver on the right, it too fell with no resistance. However, my father erased all further doubt when he reached across his body with his left hand to move his right hand and forearm off the blanket so that he could push the covers off of himself. Everyone in the room watching my basic examination recognized that he had no use of his right upper extremity. We all understood its significance. I told my mother and my sister who had hardly left my father's side during that day what would have been obvious earlier in a more clinical setting like an emergency room—my dad had had a large left-sided stroke that affected his speech center, caused his seizures, and paralyzed his right side. My mother would later say that she was glad that my father never woke to find out he could not move his right side.

In spite of this massive stroke, we believed that my father never left us completely, because he continued to exhibit the behaviors with which we had become familiar for months before the stroke. The behaviors seemed to have been so imprinted on his physiology and central nervous circuits that the serious disturbance to the higher centers of his brain seemed only to exaggerate them. There were times that he went from lying to sitting three or four times in ten minutes. Five minutes before he died, when in a physiologically state of overdrive, something in him demanded that he sit up on the side of the bed. Perhaps, the lower centers of his brain continued to respond to the bone pain and activated the neural pathways that caused him to change position. For months, he could not lie directly on his back for long periods of time without experiencing pain, so he constantly had to shift positions.

During this final day, we did not really try to understand why these behaviors kept occurring. We merely took it for granted that as long as he was with us, he would continue to do what he had always done. The behaviors kept us connected to much more than his cycle of pain; they kept us connected to his being, his essence—they were as essential as anything he could have said. The familiar behaviors embodied hope itself.

Between episodes of heightened activity, there was a long span when my father seemed to sleep deeply and comfortably. His breathing, when it was relatively easy and regular, brought a peaceful respite to all of us who hovered around his bedside. We could be certain that at least he was not suffering. I assumed, at first, that the "restful" sleep was the post-ictal aftermath of his seizures while the scrambled neurotransmitters in his brain re-established a functional balance. The physician assistant, who kept referring to my father as a geriatric patient (a designation that for some reason had never occurred to me as I considered him an ageless virulent man sapped of all his energy and youth by consumptive prostate cancer), stated that the post-ictal period in geriatric patients could sometimes last a long time. When I said over 12 hours, he responded, "Sometimes, over 24 hours."

As I watched my father's more restful state, I knew that it deprived him of fluids and nourishment. Nevertheless, the peaceful state, at first, engendered optimism, and I found myself hoping that it might continue until he became arousable. Then, when he woke, we could offer him his hard-boiled egg and possibly have a couple weeks of final conversations with him. At the point it became clear that he most likely had a massive left-sided stroke, I was less certain about the cause of the restful state and its potential duration, but I was still glad to see it, for everyone's sake.

The period of relative peacefulness allowed all of us to relax and consider a few of our own daily needs. I thought that it might be possible for my wife and me to slip in a walk on a sunny, mild Cincinnati winter day. Even my mom, who hardly left my father's side, encouraged me to take the opportunity. It was already mid-afternoon and I still had not washed my face, showered, or brushed my teeth. I still wore the same cotton undershirt and pair of oversized sweatpants that dragged beneath my heels, the same ones I had found finally in the early morning darkness of our bedroom. My brother and his wife, who had made the problematic quest for the Dilantin pills, seized the opportunity to go home and freshen up before returning around dinner. My mother, whose countenance wore dark storm clouds of worry all day, tried to rest quietly beside my father, never sleeping, but experiencing a more peaceful gentle breeze. My sister, also by his side all day, remained vigilant, but seemed more at ease.

All the in-laws, my wife, my brother-in-law, and my sister-in-law, assumed their roles of support masterfully for their concerned and grieving spouses. They floated between my father's room, the kitchen, and the den on the opposite side of the house, wherever they thought they could be most useful. My brother-in-law first turned the TV on in the kitchen to watch the NFL playoff games, first Pittsburgh eking a victory over the Indianapolis Colts and then Carolina surprising the Chicago Bears. Recognizing that my father would have had the games on, we turned the TV on in his bedroom, on mute.

Only my youngest sister, who lived the furthest away in

New Jersey, had not yet arrived on the scene. She had first heard about my father's change in condition at 8 AM, was on the earliest flight she could get between Newark and Cincinnati. At that period, there seem to be little reason to believe she would not make it before my father drew his last breath

****

No physician likes to give an opinion about how much time a person with a terminal illness has to live, but the question always comes up. The question presents a no-win proposition. The chances of being right on the mark are not nearly as good as predicting the delivery date of a pregnancy, and yet a reasonable estimate is just as critical, if not more so. If a physician underestimates the time left, he runs the risk of needing to wipe egg off his face when the patient doubles or triples his estimate, and of instilling undue alarm, promoting premature grief, and ultimately, of robbing the family of hope. The downside of overestimating the time left does not seem to be as steep. A longer period seems to offer hope, and because no one is ever prepared for the final breath of a loved one, the shock of it is not all that much greater if a person does not last as long as the estimate.

When a physician makes his estimate, there are so many variables to take into consideration that make the task almost impossible, so he is best off giving a window of time, and warning his patient about the unreliability of such estimates in the first place. He serves his patients best by telling them to take care of those things that require their health and alertness early on, and then to live each day to the extent that their health will allow. Of course, it is not always that simple, because difficult decisions hinge on a more precise estimate of the amount of time left, for example, whether or not to get Hospice involved, an organization which theoretically asks the physician to state that the patient has less than six months to live. An example more relevant to my father's situation had already arisen that day when we as the family had to decide whether to put our loved one in the hospital or keep him at home for the last hours or days of his life. We had decided to keep him at home, but if he survived longer than a day or two, and the agony and care was extended, the decision might have become increasingly problematic. Finally, what physician can avoid adjusting his estimate based upon something as unscientific as the reaction of the family to the first estimate? So it is a no-win situation around a fundamental question that is sometimes more in God's hands than in any other.

With respect to my father, I recall making my first informed estimate about how long he would live shortly after we discovered that his prostate cancer had metastasized to many of his bones in September 2004. My grim first impression was tempered by my research that suggested that the average prostate cancer patient lived about 18 months after the discovery cancer in his bones. My father, however, had symptoms consistent with bony metastases for months, but had not done the tests to confirm it; so in my own mind, I adjusted for this circumstance, but planted the 18 months in my mother's mind anyway. At the time, this seemed like a sufficiently long enough period, and if it turned out to be a low estimate, 18 months for my 76-year-old father still seemed a reasonable length of time to live. Of course, the estimate did not take into account his quality of life, and the losses that come along with accelerated dying, some substantial, others less so, losses that occurred when my father was no longer able to work 11 months after the discovery of metastases nor leave the house 13 months after.

The timing of his death came up again poignantly when my wife and I visited Cincinnati in early December 2005, about 15 months after the discovery of metastatic disease. By that time, my father was mainly bedridden, getting up for meager meals and rarely to watch a Cincinnati sports team. (That weekend, my brother and I, mainly my brother, wired a television into his room). He had given up showers, for the most part, and brushing his teeth because of the awful distorted taste of toothpaste. He doddered around the house in his skivvies, sometimes pulled low enough to reveal the top of the crease of his buttocks, to alleviate the pressure on the cancer-ridden prominences of his pelvic girdle. Because of his Tarzan garb, as I liked to call it, he was humiliated to walk around the house in front of the female spouses and grandchildren, narrowing his circle of visitors. But this weekend, when tottering the path between his bed and the kitchen, he did manage to wear loose sweat pants. He had given up talking on the phone to anyone other than his children, but our notoriously long phone calls had dwindled to a few sentences before fatigue overwhelmed him. It was at this stage of his illness that my oldest son called to get my opinion about what his grandfather's status would be during his upcoming trip to Israel.

In my earlier conversations with my oldest son, I had indicated that my father might not make it to his 77th birthday, December 21, about a week before my son's planned departure for his international trip that included 4 days at the concentration camps in Poland followed by a 12 or 13 day stay in Israel. By the time of our visit to Cincinnati, it seemed relatively certain that my father would make it to his birthday, but I believed there was a reasonable likelihood that he would die during the two weeks of his travel. My son was not satisfied with "reasonable"; his exacting, scientific mind needed a number to grasp. I offered something like forty percent that he might die, downgrading it from as high as 50%

at one point, never getting the probability low enough to make my older son comfortable about going without having a contingency plan to depart Israel emergently if his grandfather died. I told him, however, that if he went, he should complete his trip under all circumstances, rather than cutting it short and flying home. He did not like this notion either, so he decided to get his grandmother's opinion.

Throughout the ordeal of caring for my father, my mother, even while dealing with her own health issues, had taken care of everything bravely, matter-of-factly, and with amazing care and love, keeping her grief private. But for this conversation, she took the phone sobbing and determined. She told my oldest son that he could not plan his life around these things (illness and the possibility of death) and that he should not miss out on this opportunity. Her entire thrust was that he should live life and not be controlled by death, because somebody's death would always be around the corner, and life was too short. I thought that she was compelling, having grown up hearing this sort of philosophy all my life, but she apparently did not convince my commitment-and-family-oriented older son. I heard her say, "I want you to promise me that you will go and stay there." When she did not get the answer she wanted, she kept repeating, "Promise me…, promise me." Finally, when she found my son recalcitrant, she said, "If you don't promise me, I am going to give the phone to Grandpa and he will tell you to go." She believed that this threat would put an end to my son's resistance, but when he persisted, she repeated the threat a couple of more times before she walked across the house to my father's room and gave him the telephone.

Though my father's room was fifty feet away on the other side of the house, we were able to hear every word he spoke to my son through a baby monitor we used to keep track of my father when we were out of the room. My father had his own mind about everything until the end, and on this matter, it was no different. He wanted to comply with my mother's wishes to convince my son, but his life's philosophy did not completely align with my mother's, built much more on family and duty, and less on self-realization. He told my son that he should go to Israel, because he was going to be fine while he was there, that he should not worry. He did not mention dying at all, as that was something he never spoke about out loud. He spoke no more than three or four sentences before he gave the phone back to my sobbing mother, who then brought the phone back to the den so that I could complete my conversation with my son. My father remained upset after the conversation. He said, "Why are you asking me to make such decisions? I can't tell him that I want him to go. Of course I want him here!" I remember him yelling these things loud enough that I believed I heard them travel from his room, down the long hallway, through the voluminous dining room, and through the double doors, before filling the den with their anguish. Only in retrospect now do I realize that I must have heard them over the monitor.

On this final Sunday, I was again asked to offer an opinion about how long he would live, because everyone who cared about him was trying to grapple with how long he would have to suffer like this. "Length of suffering" was at the core, not as much, "how much time will we have with him." Before answering the "length" part of the concern, I thought it was important to address the "suffering" part of the concern. With as much certainty as the "son" part of me would allow, I tried to reassure them that he was not experiencing pain in his unconscious state. Furthermore, I tried to reassure them that starvation, especially when consuming food caused so much discomfort, was not painful. Each of us came to terms with this fact, that my father would more than likely never swallow another bite of food or drink another sip of water. Each of us had to overcome the instinct to provide nourishment and fluids by some means, and to accept that the most humane action to take, in this situation, was to let nature takes its course. In spite of this, my mother still recalled the example of my father's father living for over a year after his massive stroke left him bedridden and unable to speak or understand. I explained to my mother what would have been obvious to her if she were not so overwhelmed by the avalanche of the day's events—that my grandfather had been able to eat and drink and had not already been weakened by end stage prostate cancer. Finally, I offered the opinion, which did not seem bold at the time, that given my father's state of weakness before the stroke from cancer, malnutrition, dehydration, and probable kidney failure, and given the probability that he would not eat or drink again, he would not likely live for more than forty-eight hours. I recall that this short duration may have upset my sister and my sister-in-law, and I hedged up to a week. My wife also told me later that I retrieved her from our Cincinnati bedroom with the statement, "I think my father is dying," meaning imminently, sometime in the next few hours.

Still, I was operating under the assumption, and perhaps most of us were, that the greatest probability was that my father would last two more days, and that it was highly unlikely that he would live for a week, and that while it might be a blessing if he were to die sooner than two days, it was not given much consideration. So we had to prepare for giving his medications in his rectum for 2 days, changing his adult diapers for two days, managing his pain for two days, providing around the clock manpower for two days to move his emaciated frame if necessary, and most importantly, we had to prepare for watching the last little bit of life leave my father and what that might look like.

****

While my father was resting quietly in what appeared to be painfree sleep, we were briefly lulled into the belief that my father would last these two days and that it might be tolerable for us to watch this silent sleep until we could say, as it is frequently said, "He died in his sleep." But this break was a mere kindness, one among many, that my father gave us before something consumed the last little bit of life left in him. Though there is no way he could have heard our two day assessments, his spirit must have determined that sleeping for two days was no way to spend the last bit of his life's energy. One could crawl like a snail to cover a kilometer in two days or sprint like a triathlon athlete. His spirit decided upon the latter.

I do not recall my father's transition from quiet breathing to the frantic one that most humans would not achieve even if chased by a tiger from the Washington Monument to the Lincoln Memorial. Perhaps, it crept up gradually like the before noon sun or perhaps, I diverted myself with a couple of plays in the Carolina-Bears game. But it seemed that at about the same time, my mother, my sister, and I noticed that my father was breathing like a boiler working on overdrive about to explode. I imagined, alleviating my own unease, that my father's injured respiratory center in his brainstem had lost control and was driving my father to breath like a breakneck locomotive. Alternatively, I thought that he might be withdrawing from months of the regular use of narcotics, but it seemed less likely since it had only been five hours since I had inserted his Oxycontin and it should have lasted eight.

But I could not help but see the change primarily through the eyes of my mother and sister who equated his mounting agitation with suffering. He had become sweaty and moved his left limbs more, constantly brushing his left hand across his forehead as if shooing a fly or relieving an itch. I remembered that this sort of apparent agitation was difficult for nurses to watch, even veteran ones, who saw it all the time and probably had far more experience with it than I did, as I work more with the living before they reach their dying moments. Many times, I had given orders over the phone for a sedative like Ativan or Morphine to reduce this sort of agitation, even though I knew it was providing more comfort for the observer than it did for the patient.

I noticed that desperation crept into my mother's countenance again. Both my sister and my mother spoke gentle and comforting words to my father, who would not have heard them even if he were awake because of his profound loss of hearing. Yet, it seemed the natural and appropriate thing to do, and it had as great a likelihood of calming him down as what I hoped to accomplish with a couple of drugs in the Hospice emergency kit. I took a tablet of Ativan and crushed it with a mortar and pestle and mixed it with a couple drops of water. I then inserted the Ativan paste in the pooled saliva between his right gum and cheek, the side of his mouth weakened by his Korean War injury. Though I gave it hardly any time to calm him, when his overdrive state did not abate, I gave him 10 mg of a concentrated morphine solution in the same place. We still did not get the desired result, the same restful state that had comforted us an hour earlier. To my dismay, the side of his mouth that had so easily admitted my finger now allowed the pool of saliva to run out the side of his mouth, and with it, an unknown quantity of the medication. What's worse, it turned my father's lips into a raspy wet baffle with each exhalation, accentuating the sounds of suffering.

My mother called the Hospice nurse and then handed

the phone to me. I explained the change in my father's condition and what I had tried to alleviate it. I asked her for suggestions. She had no suggestions right away, but she did say something to which I gave very little weight at the time; she said that sometimes this type of agitated behavior was a terminal event. She then asked me if I had gotten orders for what I had done from my father's managing caregiver, the Physician's Assistant. I imagine that from her perspective, as part of an organization closely monitored by Medicare, she could not ignore standard procedure, even when a father under the care of his physician-son is in physiologic agony near the end of his life. Nevertheless, I told her that I was familiar with both medications that I had given, and furthermore, I told her how I intended to use even more without further orders. Nonplussed, she told me that she would discuss my father's conditions with the physician assistant and call back with the necessary orders and to see how my father was doing.

My father was still agitated when I got off the phone with the Hospice nurse. His eyes were open, wild-eyed and unseeing, and his left hand was no long reaching for his forehead, but was grabbing for the edge of the bed. At first, we tried to thwart what appeared to be an effort to pull himself to a seated position on the edge of the bed. We tried to reason with a mind that had not responded for 8 hours in any discernible way to the most basic of statements and questions. When his efforts continued, we had no choice but to augment them. We helped him to a seated upright position on the edge of the bed, and I placed myself to his right to prevent him from tipping to his paralyzed side. His head flopped forward so that his chin almost rested on his chest and his saliva soaked the upper half of his undershirt. I reached for a Kleenex on the night table beside the bed to dam up the stream of drool. We all spoke in comforting tones, "Do you feel better sitting up?" "Is that better?"

He had not been sitting up longer than a few minutes when I began to feel his weight shift backwards. I took this shift as an indication that he wanted (as if he still had intention) to lie down. I received no response when I asked, but I told my mother, who was sitting on the other side, and my sister, who was crouched in front of him, that I thought that he wanted to lie down. That was my hope anyway. As I withdrew my support from his right side, his head and torso did sink backwards toward the pillow. After the upper part of his body found the supine position, we lifted his legs, still draped over the edge of the bed, back into bed and arranged his body in a comfortable position beneath the sheets. (We tried to preserve his modesty, even in his unconscious state, and our comfort, as his lower half was clad only in an adult diaper.) His breathing began to slow and the terror in his eyes began to subside, as if his potboiler energy had been intended for one thing, to sit on the edge of the bed at least one more time.

Shortly after we eased my father into a supine position on the bed and watched his state of agitation begin to expend the last of its fuel, a nurse sent by Hospice to provide an eight-hour shift of assistance arrived at our home. Earlier in the day, when we decided to delay any transfer to the Hospice inpatient unit, we had also decided to put our name on the list for an eight hour shift of respite nursing care reserved for the most critical Hospice patients. We had not expected any assistance that day, as it was Sunday, and as we were new to this list. However, later we learned that a nurse had become available. One of us remarked that our luck probably had come at the expense of another Hospice patient who no longer required it, recognizing Hospice patients do not get better. Yet, when I met the nurse, I suspected that she became available for other reasons. From the moment I led her back to my father's room, I had the impression that the amount of attention that she would require from us might be more than what she could offer to my father.

She was a moving van with a Volkswagen Beetle engine, a mountain of late middle-age humanity that overwhelmed the capacity of her heart, lungs, muscles, and joints. Walking was a chore, sitting down was an adventure, and getting up was an uncertain proposition. What's more, she understood all of this, responding at one point to all our attempts to assist her by saying, "I am a pathetic human being." At her behest, I lead her back to my father's room where she received a brief set of introductions and immediately looked for a place to sit near the head of the my father's bed. But first she had to assure her safety, because once settled, she did not intend to move, especially due to a collapsed chair or one that rocked backwards. She asked, "Do you have a sturdy chair?" She accepted the card table chair folded beside the dresser before I thought to offer her a large sturdy cushioned upholstered chair with strong oak arms from the kitchen. By that time, she had lowered herself like a circus elephant on the trainer stool into the first-offered chair and kindly refused the second, "This chair will be fine. Could you get me my clipboard over there?" She recognized that she was a burden, but her battered dignity resisted the tendency to be any trouble.

Shortly after our nurse planted herself in the prime real estate at my father's head, the on-call Hospice nurse called back to deliver orders from Physician Assistant, and to get an update on my father's condition. He affirmed my management more or less. Then I turned my attention to my father for the first time since the respite nurse had arrived and settled. He seemed calmer and I was thinking that the storm had passed. I told the Hospice nurse that when he had been agitated, "He had been hyperventilating a mile a minute. Now, as I look at him, I would say he is hypoventilating. In fact, he is hardly breathing at all." I had seen this earlier in the day, so I was not thinking it was the end. But I studied him closely and continued, "In fact, I don't think that he is breathing at all."

No sooner had I uttered these words, my sister, who was at the foot of his bed, let out a long and sorrowful wail, enough for all of us and all others who had lost a loved one at that moment, and ran to her father's head, arriving with my mother from the side of the bed opposite to the anchored nurse. My mother, who had mainly grieved behind closed doors, could finally sob in my father's presence; somehow my mother and sister managed to hug each other, and my father too, in the first light of the dawn of their mourning. The Hospice nurse on the other end of the phone seemed to understand the scene in the room and released me to attend to it. Behind me, glowing and flickering in the dim light of a late winter afternoon and drawn shades, the television played the final minutes of the Carolina-Chicago game. Already, the respite nurse was expressing her sorrow for the man whom she had met less than ten minutes earlier. It seemed awkward to me, but given her role in the world, it may not have been a record for her. I cried I suppose like most men, if I can believe an article in a well know medical journal, my eyes filling with tears, my nose congesting with them, and my throat closing with them, before they spilled down my cheek.

****

In my twenty plus years as a family physician, I had naturally encountered the recently lifeless bodies of patients I had come to know, but I do not recall ever observing their very last breaths, and of course, none of them was my father. I therefore had as little idea as the next person what it would be like to be present at the moment when the final remnant of hope was extinguished that my father would ever wake up and look at his loved ones with eyes of familiarity; I had little idea what it would be like to be present at the moment my father's physical presence would of necessity vanish eternally. I understood instinctively, at a minimum, that death meant these things. Though I was not shocked by his expiration at that moment, I was surprised by it, because we had not planned on it for at least a couple of days. An hour earlier, it had seemed safe for my brother to take a breather at home and we had seemed certain that my younger sister from New Jersey had plenty of time to arrive before her father's final breath. Caught by surprise, I did not feel an overwhelming sense of relief, though at some level, I knew we were spared hours of possible agitation and waiting; his ship went under suddenly instead of slowly sinking. I suppose without a tinge of self-consciousness, I simultaneously felt a spontaneous surge of grief and of epiphanous realization—this is what it is like to know that the only father you will ever have has left the physical realm; it was a horrible honor and privilege, a profound paradox, to be present for an event even rarer and more momentous than a birth.

The respite nurse, from her chair, leaned over my father with her stethoscope and confirmed the absence of a heartbeat. As a matter of courtesy and respect, she asked me if I would like to perform my own examination. Though I could see my father's death mask from the foot of the bed, somehow I thought that it was something my father would have wanted me to do. He usually wanted my medical opinion above any other; he valued my advice except on those matters in which he did not seek an opinion in the first place. Before putting the stethoscope to his chest, I put my hand on his chest because I wanted him to know that even though his heart was not beating that I knew he had a giant one and that I was his son honoring him, and my putting a stethoscope to his chest was a privilege for me, and one of the last rites I could perform for him as his physician son.

After she confirmed my father's death on her checklist of things to do, the respite nurse on her third attempt arose from her chair to take care of the necessary paperwork and make the necessary phone calls. She declined any assistance when I started to the chair to help her up and when I asked her if she needed help finding the kitchen. Before leaving the room, she asked us if we wanted her to clean my father up. We had no idea, at the time, that this was standard practice and wondered why she thought we would allow someone who barely knew my father to do something as intimate as cleaning him up, especially recognizing his extreme modesty when he was breathing. After finally reaching her feet, she uttered with self-disgust, "I am a pathetic human being." I felt sorry for her plight, to be thrust in the midst of an unknown grieving family, knowing that her immensity dominated everyone's first impression, knowing that any family had to wonder if she was going to expire before the patient, and then, to have the misfortune to leave on this first impression, before she had time to let her humanity and spirit leave the final, lasting impression. Our compassionate natures felt all of this, but we were glad when the invited intruder was no longer part of what was becoming a sacred family communion.

So many times, a Hospice nurse has notified me that one of my patients "passed away peacefully" at such-and-such-a-time. But I never considered how others died who did not warrant this hackneyed description. I recall an incident shortly after I learned to drive. I took a short cut through the sprawling grounds of a Cincinnati mental institution called Longview Hospital. A baby rabbit charged in my path and I heard the thump of the tires pass over it. I had traveled 50 yards or so before I had the courage to look back. To my horror, it was flopping around, flipping high into the air frontward and backwards, as if its terminal agony had destroyed its bearings in relation to the earth. All urbanites have heard of chickens running around after they are decapitated. These are not peaceful deaths. My father did not "pass away peacefully." He seemed to distill all his terror into a short period that consumed his last bit of life. Only then did he find a peace, even more profound in contrast to the battle before. What words, I wonder, would a Hospice nurse have used to describe my father's final moments?

****

My father's time of death was 4:20 PM. We did not let the undertaker's assistants have him until around 8:30 PM. In part, we were just not ready to let him go, but mainly we needed to express the love that rose to the surface, no longer submerged by our concern about how much pain he was in, whether he would eat his next meal, or when he should take his next pills; it was rich and pure and overflowing, alive and real, and he in this peaceful, agitation-free state to hear it and receive it, and his humility was in no condition to dismiss it. The moment was all the more remarkable because of the contrast between it and fifteen minutes earlier, our "then", the precipitous drop of class 5 rapids through a narrow channel bounded by steep canyon walls and littered with huge boulders that created sucking currents, and our "now", a placid, glassine pool cloistered by a bank of willow trees. I called my brother because I knew that he deserved and needed this time with his father. My older sister's husband left for the airport to pick up my younger sister. All the little chickens were coming home to roost one last time around their father.

I did not anticipate the intensity of my need to be with my father after he took his last breath. Before that time, had I thought about a family hovering around and touching a corpse, I would have thought it morbid and slightly pathologic. All the kind things and loving words left like flowers on the grave should have been shared while his ears still heard and his brain still perceived. But there was no remorse in our motivation to be with our father. Each of us in the weeks and months preceding his death had demonstrated in deeds our love and respect for our father. For me, it came down to this— this was the last time that I was ever going to see my father in the flesh, only one person just like him for all eternity, and that from here on out I would have to rely on my memory, photos, and dreams, and here he was yet lying with us, peaceful and still, his lips symmetric in their final peace, one of the wounds of life effaced by death; I was suspended in something beautiful, meaningful, transcendent, an extraordinary personal and family transitional moment and passage.

None of us imagined that his "spirit" was still with his body, but it could have been. Perhaps these hours helped prepare us to sever the earthly connection. We could give our personal final goodbye, and place the proper punctuation at the end of the sentence of his life. It was probably all of these things, not the least bit perverse, but the completely natural expression of our grief, the natural flow of our warmth toward this human being that was central to our lives, whose soft hands were now beginning to cool. Each of us gravitated to different parts of his body to receive its natural balm before rotating to the next. I do not know how many times I traced out the bottom of his rib cage, made so much more prominent by months of wasting that returned him to the trim weight of his youth. In this restful state, he was no longer "the disease" that had stolen pleasure after pleasure from his life—at that moment, he had become for us the summation of his life. All conflict, friction and disputes in life sublimated away and what remained was sublime love and peacefulness. We could visit any moment of our lives with him from the earliest memory to his last breath with an otherworldly acceptance.

I lingered with his hands, as if I had a fetish for them, because he would attempt anything with them and they embodied his spirit as much as any other part of his body. I do not know how many times I returned to his head and gray-white hair that still had the freshly cut look of my sister's haircut a few weeks earlier, and that, in spite of the day's agitation, had only a few locks awry. With his final breath, the odor of decay that accompanied his exhalation had disappeared. Though he had not had the strength to shower for a week prior to his final day and though perspiration periodically drenched his head, a sweet, cotton candy scent wafted mysteriously from his hair. It was pure and fresh, like a meadow fully blossomed after a spring shower. His true nature, in the end, had asserted itself and percolated up through his hair. Anyone who knew my father knew he was the sweetest of men, who adopted a profession, the manufacture of preserves, which was the perfect accompaniment to his nature. From his hair, his children received this miracle to carry with them the rest of their lives.

My older sister, my brother, and I, alone, in pairs, or all in the bed together, shared my father like we were all of the same mind and body, as aware of the others' needs as we were of our own. In that moment, my father achieved a union among his children in a way it had never been possible in life. We expressed our hearts freely in front of each other. I said while running my hand along his curled soft cool hands, "I like his hands because he could do anything with them." Or tracing out his ribcage, "I love you, Dad." I recall my brother, who continued to update my father about events at work after his illness forced him to retire, asked "Who's going to ask me all the questions now?" Later, he uttered what he tried to communicate in his deeds during the months before he died,

"I don't know if I ever told you dad, but thank you." My father may not have heard these words, but they came from deep within my brother's heart. I was transported back to the brother of my childhood with whom I shared a bedroom and my early life, who was the best man at my wedding, whose successes on the football field I was as proud of as my own. My father's body refurbished old bonds, rusted by disuse, and bridged the gap created by the years of lives led separately in medicine and business. My older sister spent most of her time at my father's head; her sobs were sporadic and gentle, showery after the initial torrent. I do not recollect what she said, because her words blended in with the depth of her love already known to all of us. I had to share the experience with my wife, and she too discovered the unexpected spirituality of this time with my father. She said, "He looks so good!" No one expected the beauty that would emerge when the pain and worry left his visage.

I asked my mother, feeling slightly silly, if I could bring my old yellow lab from the basement to say his goodbyes. My father had, at first, made fast friends with the dog by slipping him food under the table, and always took great pleasure in the dog's superhuman enjoyment of our haven in northern Michigan in Suttons Bay. The dog manifested its retrieving instinct in a peculiar and hilarious way. For hours, we could throw stones into the bay behind the house and the dog would retrieve in return, after diving for up to thirty seconds, 10-pound boulders from the bottom of the bay. During a five-day span of his youth, he littered the back yard with over 200 of the algae slimed boulders. Later, as the dog aged, rather than throwing the rocks back into the bay, we piled the boulders in a planter as a living memorial to the dog. My father's delight in the dog, however, began to diminish when the dog began to ignore him, especially after he lost the energy to contend with the impersonal spunk of an aging dog. Still, at some point, I had linked the destinies of the aging lab and my father when they both became similarly slower and more fragile, and the dog surpassed my father's human years in dog years. Statistics put their final days in the same vicinity. As I ascended the stairs with the leashed dog, I feared that he would ignore my father in death as he had too often toward the end of his life, and I would feel all the more silly. But the dog brought fresh tears to my eyes when he licked the curled fingers of my father's empty hand that lay at the edge of the bed.

By the time my younger sister from New Jersey had arrived, her three siblings had already spent two or three hours saying goodbye. She had been awakened by my urgent phone call in early morning darkness and arrived after the dim light of winter dusk had passed. Her daylight had been consumed on planes and in airports. She had not been a privileged participant in the horrible drama of the day, a day that had the tempo and intensity of a birth, but with the opposite outcome. When she did finally arrive in the Cincinnati Airport, she was not met by one of the faces of her childhood, but by her newest, and dearest brother-in-law who told her that her father had died. She arrived unprimed by the drama of the day and at the periphery of its inner circle. She felt more than the rest of us this contracting window of time to speak her heart to her father. When she arrived, she therefore requested time alone with her father. She went into the room to view for the first time the aftermath of the day, and closed the door behind her. I understood her need to say her parting words alone, but I still felt somehow shut out. It temporarily changed the magic of the moment when the hearts and minds of his children seemed united. I joked in the kitchen while the door to his room remained closed, "She's got issues. That's why she needs to be alone with him." Of course, we children all had issues, but, those of us who had the privilege of lending comfort that last day, were somehow temporarily cleansed of them. When my sister emerged from the room, she too entered the magic of the inner circle of family.

After the door opened again to my father's room, I knew that the last of his children had come home to roost one last time and that I needed to prepare myself to let go of whatever my father's body had become at that moment. It was still a tangible connection to a life central to who I was, and perhaps more importantly, central to who I ought to be. His death had purified him of his faults during that period, and perhaps for all eternity. If at that moment I perceived that his body represented this connection, how could I ever let go, other than to recognize that I inevitably had to move beyond this time? Life was going to move on. We all would have to use our evolving memories of our father without the benefit of his specific sage responses and advice. We would all be left only with our imaginations and our consciences, much of it his construction, to apprehend his guidance when it was called for. And how to depart from the crescendo of affection and love during this period, all that we could not express while he was alive without mutual embarrassment? It could go on for hours, but time could not remain in this magical suspended animation; the action of life and reality had to reassert itself. But I would not call the funeral home yet to pick him up. He had to be ours for one more roost, so that we could immerse ourselves in the deep well of meaning our mutual love gave to our lives.

****

The curtain began to descend over the beautiful ballet that we performed around our father; I could no longer delay calling the funeral home to pick him up. We were all still arranged around my father in various poses when a husky man in a black overcoat, reeking of cigarettes, and a wiry woman arrived. The man spoke for the couple as consolingly as his tobacco-gruff voice and iron-worker stature could muster, first expressing his sympathy, and then allowing us as much time as we needed with our father. Considerately, they had come into the room without their gurney. At the time, I thought that they were going to somehow manually carry him out to their hearse. I had considered gurneys as vehicles of the living, though I am sure I had seen them used for the freshly dead on television. I even mentioned to my wife my hope that my brother and I might be called upon to move my father, a duty and a privilege. Also my father would have had someone familiar with him as he left his house. But when they came back into the house with the gurney, I knew that not only was the curtain just about to touch the floor, but that they also would not need me to accompany my father outside the house.

Before surrendering my father to these practiced strangers, in turn, we all kissed my father on the forehead one more time, "I love you, dad." Still speaking for the pair, the man in the trench coat asked us to leave the room. I imagined that moving an unwieldy fresh corpse could sometimes be awkward, and that they might get frustrated and handle it a bit too roughly. Or perhaps, the family might find it disturbing to watch their loved one that had been so still and peaceful suddenly obey the laws of gravity when a limb flops off the bed or the head snaps back. Anticipating our concerns, he reassured us, "We'll be careful." Then, he asked us if we preferred his head covered or uncovered when they brought him from the room. Having spent the past four hours admiring and speaking to that head, we answered with unified conviction, "Uncovered." He felt it necessary to explain that some preferred it covered. We left and they closed the door behind us.

While they loaded my father, we retrieved the suit and

tie my mother and sister had chosen earlier for his viewing in the casket. We had interpreted the funeral director's instructions to mean, "Choose the suit he would have worn to his own funeral." My mother and sisters had already occupied themselves with this task earlier while my brother and I were rekindling our childhood and tending to our emotional needs together around our father. I was drawn into the decision briefly to help choose a tie, but mainly I procured a couple of ties for myself with which I could later keep a piece of my father close to my heart. We were also told to put the undergarments on him that he would have worn on a typical day. When putting his underwear on, we removed the ridiculous pull-up diaper that he had lain in all day and displayed, with unaccustomed immodesty, to the entire world when in his agitation he kept pushing off the covers. My mom, with my brother's and my help, did clean up some minor residue before sliding on the fresh pare of underwear, the only "cleaning up" he would need. My mother said, "He told me that I was the only one to clean him up." When prepared to leave us, he was in his clean undergarments, accompanied by his rarely worn navy suit, covered in a blanket to protect him from the winter chill. We sent his glasses because that is the way my mother remembered him. When he passed us in the hallway, his face was still serene, unaffected by his loved ones lined up at the entrance to the kitchen grasping at second-to-last glimpses. We hardly took a breath while two strangers, faces etched with appropriate gravity, wheeled our father from our lives.

    When my father's body left the house, I anticipated that his absence from the room would become a huge presence. The room had been a guest bedroom, mainly used when my younger sister's family visited, or when my wife and I came with one or both of our children. But when my father's sleep became extremely fitful from his insidious, incessant pain, and my mother's sleeping pattern began to clash with his own, disrupting both of their well-beings, my father began to spend his nights plodding back and forth between his matrimonial bed and the guest bed. Finally, a couple of months before he was wheeled away forever, he began to live in the room. He could be found in the room, lying in the bed or sitting on it playing his handheld Yatzee game, unless he was in the kitchen finishing off a frosty from Wendy's or making one of his hopeful trips to the bathroom (hopeful that his draining efforts would be rewarded). By the time he departed, he had spent more time in that room than everyone else who visited combined. The room was no longer a guest bedroom, nor was it the bedroom where he died, but it was a place much like the sacred grounds where venerable old elephants in Tarzan movies went to find comfort and die in peace. It had become not only a sad place, but also a room filled with mysticism and eternity.

I returned to this room that no longer housed the human being that made it sacred. As I anticipated, in that empty bed with blanket and sheet awry, I experienced the first inkling of the void my father's absence would create. (The room was transformed, in some ways like the bed in a hospital room that has just lost its occupant to a fatal disease; the empty rumpled sheets and unattached IV's contain the story of losing battle, but also foreshadow a different purpose when the next patient arrives.) The plastic case on the dresser still contained my father's medications, but I found the narcotics and relaxing medications conspicuously absent, confiscated by the Hospice nurse so that a drug abusing family member would not use them. The room reeked of cigarette smoke, an obnoxious gift left behind by the funeral attendant. Unlike the wisteria of my father's hair that took us into a sublime realm, it brought a bar room or a pool hall into the room. Life goes on; the secular mingles with the sacred.

I wondered whether my mom would be able to face the

emptiness in the room. She was able to confront it head on, much as she had many of the aspects of my father's illness. She enlisted my help to remove the old sheets and pad that was wet from an episode of incontinence; we replaced it with a fresh one. Later on, when I returned to the room to begin to accustom myself to the void, I found the bed made with a bedspread that it had not seen for weeks. The room was beginning to feel more like the occasionally used guest bedroom, a reminder that life goes on in spite of the death of an individual and that <u>the sacred exists only</u> in contrast to our <u>predominantly secular existence</u>.

****

Even before my father died, I accepted the responsibility of giving a eulogy. Months earlier, I had begun to write down my thoughts and on one occasion tried to turn some of these ideas, unsuccessfully, into distinct paragraphs. My incomplete musings do not seem so tortured now, and they do paint a portrait of the man that inspired them; so I will share them:

"One weekend, a few months before he left us in body, my father was lured outdoors by his friend Pablo who was finishing a retaining wall of stones on the steep hill beside his home. Accompanying him outdoors, I noticed along the walk at the top of the hillside that there were several boulders that were similar in composition to ones I had taken from the beach at Suttons Bay. The only difference was, there were a couple of the size that I had left behind, because they were too heavy to carry. One especially, flat speckled granite and as large as an elephant ear, seemed impossible for one man to carry. So I asked him, "Are these boulders from Suttons Bay." Yes they were. "Well, how did you get them back to

Cincinnati." I carried them. Remembering my reluctance to tackle such boulders, I asked, "By yourself?" And with an iota of disgust for the frail state his disease had left him, he said, "You forget that I was not always as I am now."

"I had forgotten the quiet virile man before his anti-testosterone prostate cancer medications stole his muscles. I had forgotten that my father at 60 had more strength than I have ever had or ever will have. I had forgotten that this was the man who in his thirties thought nothing of emptying several one hundred pound sugar bags in a kettle of boiling water while making preserves. I had forgotten that he was the one who at sixty, while helping my brother and I construct a planter along a six foot high concrete wall at Suttons Bay as a protective barrier for his grandchildren, had himself lost his balance, only to land gracefully, knees slightly bend on a flat surfaced rock below, sticking the landing like an Olympic gymnast hurdling off the high bar. Here was the grandfather version of the eighth grader who broke the Hughes High School 50 yard dash record with a 5.8 second effort, putting so much into it that he, legend has it, that he dislocated his hip. Barred from playing football by his mother, he went on to be a champion discus thrower. He was not a strutting rooster with his strength; it was what he needed to get the job done."

"I can remember a time, when like most teenage boys I lost sight of the virtues of my father. I mention this now only because this period contrasts so dramatically with the admiration that I later developed for my father. I learned that the qualities I cherish most in myself descended, in part, directly from him. I thanked God that I was subjected to his work ethic, his generosity, his ability to listen, his humility and his love for family. Knowing that he was my father made me feel better about myself, because I carried some of him inside of me. That he dressed in a t-shirt and cotton work pants and worked with the laboring men he employed no longer was an embarrassment, but a shield of honor."

"Some men may espouse equality, but my father practiced it in a way that most likely never will. He worked alongside Rufus, Norris, and Arthur, for years, performing many of the same arduous tasks that they did to make a batch of jam. Not only did he lead these men by his example, throwing 100 pound sugar bags around and enduring the Cincinnati summer heat and humidity amplified by hot kettles, developing the back of an 80 year old by the age of 40, he understood every nut, bolt and cog of the function of his jelly business, from the ingredients of every product made to the inner working of the kettles and laborers. While I did not appreciate it at the time, I learned about responsibility when I accompanied him, somewhat begrudgingly, on some Sundays to take the fruit from the freezer for the next day's cookings."

I loved and respected my father, yet I was unable to focus on what I loved most about him because I kept stumbling on the complexity of the man and the complexity of my relationship with him as it evolved through childhood and adulthood. At the time, I had no idea that it might be impossible to write a eulogy about a person before he dies, because one can't see the forest for the trees. What I loved most about my father only came into clear focus after I discovered what it was I would miss the most after he was gone.

The eulogy that I delivered two days later turned out to be more of a group project among my siblings than I anticipated. I may have written every word of it, but after their input, I deleted nearly as many words as I delivered. In my original version, I could not ignore that some of my father's acts of kindness, though pure in their intent, complicated the lives of his family. Without stating it, I was most fascinated by the deeds in which his strengths merged with his weaknesses, those acts of kindness that combined his caring about others with an inability to say "no" to a decent fellow human being in need. I alluded to a fundamental irony in his politics. I said that my father may have voted for Bush and was certainly one of his thousand points of light, but he cared more for the everyday man than most democrats. I was trying to say that my father's behavior toward others really transcended politics. When I wrote the lines, I knew that I might be disregarding the funereal audience, but I felt that I needed to demonstrate that my father took risks in his acts of kindness and that my father was living evidence that there are big-hearted staunch republicans in the world.

However, my siblings recognized that a eulogy is supposed to put the deceased to rest, not create unrest among the living. My brother justified my deletions by speaking up for my father and putting himself in the shoes of the funereal audience. I fumed for a bit after the criticisms, but that is the nice thing about the word document—once a line is deleted, it is like it never existed. For a period, I felt like I removed all the color and seasoning from the eulogy, that it was bland and trite. Still, when practicing it, there were many lines in it that brought tears to my eyes and caused me to choke. With each practice, I got further and further through it before I choked until finally, after seven tries, I worked all the way through it without interruption. After I delivered the eulogy, my brother, who had been most pained by the inappropriate color of the earlier draft, moved to tears, thanked me. It was what he wanted to hear. No doubt, the words that follow, though they ring with truth, would have made my father shrink in his chair or leave the room. He had to be silenced forever before we could really sing his praises with him in the room.

The Eulogy:

"I share with my father an innate reticence in front of larger audiences, but if he were in my shoes today and I in his, he would be up here. He would offer a few eloquent words and would ask no more for himself, because he was a man of few words, a man that at his core operated from a few basic, simple values. He was a good, generous, hard-working, family man. He was an immensely proud man with enormous humility, traits that instilled in him a strong desire to help others with just as strong a hesitation to accept it. It allowed him to appreciate goodness wherever it existed— in his friends and family, but also in his employees, who he viewed as his work family, his car mechanic, the salvage yard worker, the plumber, the fruit packing plant owner, or the checkout woman at Costco's. His standards could be high, but his subsequent loyalty and perseverance for some of these people was remarkable. Rufus, one of his original employees at Cincinnati Preserving Company, were he here today, would attest to this. For years after Rufus retired, my father visited him many Sundays, one time delivering an air conditioner during a particularly hot Cincinnati summer. He never missed seeing him in the hospital when he suffered a complication of his diabetes and when the time came, he sat among his family at his funeral. He did not have to get involved; it was his nature. He was always thinking about others, until the end— while he did not want to share his plight with anyone other than his immediate family, the intensity of his concern for others never wavered. My dad never complained about the steep decline in his health, never saw that death was right around the corner, hardly winced when moving from lying to sitting in bed was pure agony and swallowing the last bite of eggs pure torture (even smothered in mayonnaise); he abided it all because he still had a breath to care about someone else. I had thought in my informed naiveté, having accompanied many of my patients to the other side, that it was a fear of death that kept him going, but all along, it was the drive to live for the love of others."

"I thank my father for his example of generosity. To be raised in the circle of his immediate family was truly a place of milk and honey. He had the uncanny ability of recognizing a need in our lives before we knew it existed. While for my brothers and sisters, living in this Promised Land offered something just as substantial and helpful, for me, it was a steady stream of hardly used, well maintained vehicles (making me the envy of everyone who works with me). Yes, I agree that material things and money are not the only constituents of generosity, in fact, at times being stingy can be an act of generosity and love. But my father was a natural giver; he was not a taker. I do not think that he considered what he was doing as anything but a natural act of love and care for his children. I learned early on in my relationship with my father about the great satisfaction he received in his acts of generosity. It became so much easier to accept his gifts, and in return, give him everything that he really wanted without demanding, my unconditional love and respect."

"Besides his family, my father's life was his work. Growing up watching my father's commitment to his work was among the most important aspects of our education. When we were young, he believed the best way to instill a good work ethic was to be a disciplinarian and a believable enforcer. So this gentle soul adopted a gruff exterior (We all saw through the ruse by the time we were teenagers). Nightly, he had my brother and me competing for the most push-ups. We both did between 50 and 100; only perfect ones counted. My wiry younger brother usually reached the higher pinnacle first, only to end up on his hindquarters in our one-on-one tackle games in our living room. Older brothers always have the advantage, that is, until being older becomes a disadvantage. While I remember these times more fondly than one might suspect, I do not think that we children developed our work ethic from doing push-ups, and from the fear of the stick. It was from watching him do what amounted to his daily push-ups, lifting one hundred pound sugar bags and pouring them into the kettle or taking fruit from the freezer on Sundays for the next day's cooking or creating a new or better flavor for a jam. Our classroom was his commitment to the daily operation of a small business, finding no task too menial, even on the most sultry, summer Cincinnati days."

"By now all of you who shared my father's life must know who lay at the center of his universe, who provided its sunrises, a new morning even at the end of his days on earth — it was his family, his wife, his children and their spouses, and his grandchildren. Well, dad, I am here today to tell you that the feeling is mutual. We will remember you whose greatest pleasure in life was to watch one of his children enjoying the company of another. We will remember you who even while dying willed a greater cohesion and love in his family by demonstrating a heroic love for them. Dad, you will remain at the center of our universe and we will remember you in our sunrises and sunsets yet to come."

AFTERWORD

The dreams in which I visit my father, including a farfetched adventure in an abandoned warehouse, are coming less frequently than they did five years ago. I do not need a tree, as I did for Izzy, to remind me that he once was an integral part of my life. The better parts of his nature, particularly his generosity to good souls from all walks of life, continue to inhabit me. His example has infected my wife and my sons as well, as they no doubt dedicate noble deeds in his remembrance. His being is embedded in the matrix of my brain, both genetically and from intimate familiarity, and it has formed a fundamental connection to centers of joy and satisfaction; when I behave in a way that recalls his finer moments, I feel his presence and I feel complete, if just for a moment.

The Izzy Memorial, the long planter full of rocks in Suttons Bay Michigan, has been dismantled, for the most part, and put to better use. The rocks with which Izzy once wandered the yard in victory laps, until he could be coaxed to drop them, have been cherry-picked and moved to South Haven where they form the border of a bean-shaped garden just in front of Izzy's dogwood. At least in theory, the odds have been increased for an errant rock molecule to reunite materially and spiritually with one from Izzy. I still visit the dogwood tree in the shady back of our yard from time to time. The tree seems destined to recapitulate the behavior of the dog it is commemorating. After blossoming the first year, it has grown 3 feet in all directions, but it has not blossomed since. Like Izzy it might be reserving its most appealing behavior for the beginning of its second decade with us. We are partly to blame, just as we were with Izzy's behavior; with Izzy, we could have been as consistent as we were earnest in his training, and for the dogwood, we might have chosen a more convivial place, not at the edge of a dense wood of pine, oak, sassafras, and maple, with large overshadowing oaks in front. Still, my hope is that before I need to bury another dog, it will express some of Izzy's spirit in spring quartets of white petals.

It is not difficult to envision that I will soon be confronted with another failing parent. My mother is no longer the vibrant matriarch capable of planning and executing a holiday meal for 15 or 16 of matzo ball soup, brisket and chicken, 2 baked casseroles, 2 vegetables, oven baked potatoes perfectly browned and seasoned, cherry Jell-O with all the fixings—little marshmallows, bananas and apples—and deserts from every compartment of Cincinnati's Graeters, doubling the calories of what preceded it. In part, she suffers from the absence of my father, always in the background of such an effort. But she has had a series of medical issues that have nipped at her memory, her strength, and her emotional and physical stamina. If she were a patient of mine, I would certainly encourage family involvement in her care and oversight in her safety. What stamina she does have is often consumed by phone calls with friends less stalwart with their ailments than she is, and by some anxiety about all the new sensations that she is experiencing with the ailments of aging. Yet she remains able to revert to a version of the timeless mother, allowing me to become the timeless son, when suddenly she becomes that person I want most to share my thoughts and feelings in absolute safety.

Living over three hundred miles away, I do not know whether I will be there at the moment of her deliverance, when the last little corner of her sun slips below the horizon. I do not know where her sun is on the horizon right now. She is not one to demand my attention and make it known where she is. I must use my own judgment. But I suspect that I need to dive in or I will miss some important moments. A wonderful person will be reborn at the moment the horizon eclipses her sun, the person who accepted me unconditionally while I found my way out of the blind alleys and punishing losses of my life, and I will carry this spirit with me along side my father.

Jessie, the gentle, tennis ball obsessed Chocolate Lab that succeeded Izzy has crossed into the afternoon years of life. He is yet minimally grizzled and in dog years, only 52, but there are moments already when I am wary of the end. During these moments, I get a familiar brick in my chest, but I do not foresee the level of suffering I experienced in the wake of Izzy's death. I was blindsided by the end and the degree of pain associated with letting him go. I was completely immersed in the details of Izzy's dying care and did not prepare myself for the end until the very end. More importantly, I had not realized how unconditionally, naively, and completely I had insinuated him into my daily existence.

I have not checked the nature of my heart with Jessie

merely to avoid this pain (when I am home for a couple of day he stares at me with dreamy eyes wondering about my next move). I do not look forward to the eternal absence of his loyal, joyful, and benevolent presence, and as painful as it was to let go of Izzy the way I did it, if given the opportunity, I would take a similar course with Jessie. I would give up my comfort for his comfort and joy at the end, hold him during his final moment, and bury him beneath an Appalachian flowering tree like a dogwood or a redbud (but in a sunnier spot) to hold his spirit.

The experience will be different and it will be the same. It should not have the immensity and the intensity of the first time, and as much as they both embody the canine spirit, they are different dogs-- Izzy was Sylvester and Jessie is Tweety Bird. But I will make the passage once again arm in arm with my equally concerned and involved wife while Lake Michigan sunsets form the backdrop. After he is gone, when the silence becomes too deafening, no excitement of clamoring claws on wood floors, no flapping ears signaling morning's arrival, no insistent barks to throw a tennis ball, we will fill our house again with a canine spirit.

I struggled in "On Human and Canine Bonds" with identifying the exact nature of the dog's role in the family, not so much with the comparisons I made between a pre-kindergarten child and an aging parent, but with comparing the loss of either of these family members with the loss of a dog. The loss of a dog can be very painful; in my medical practice, I have seen it precipitate a period of human depression. Yet I now believe that after the loss of a dog, there comes a period which nearly heals the wound. The bonding with another dog and another canine spirit can be an important part of this healing process, but I suspect the process might proceed to completion even without another dog, as human to human bonds fill in the open wound. On the other hand, when a child or a spouse dies, unlike a dog, the gaping wound rarely heals; it is a singular wound. Everything might heal around it so that it is barely visible to onlookers, perhaps even to the individual who has sustained the loss, but the wound is never so deeply buried that some smell, some holiday event, some song, some nostalgic breeze does not briefly awaken the loss. Being human, loving and caring about others, human or otherwise, will always make us vulnerable to all kinds of wounds. We are all among the walking wounded. Only our continued capacity to love, create, connect, and produce allows us to continue this challenge we call life.

I have the sunsets of loved ones yet to go in my life. We all do, whether we want them or not, whether we choose to view them in their entirety or not; their sun will still linger, sometimes endlessly, on the horizon, before disappearing and returning a remarkable glow for all those who stayed until the end. We will dive into some, because we must, and into others, because there is no one else to do it. We will simultaneously mourn the passing of life and celebrate its existence; we will savor it and choke on it. When it is over, we will feel worn and empty, but more wholly human, with the hope that we will not soon have to dive into one again. We will inhabit the world of the walking wounded as long as it is our destiny. But we need not worry about enduring the end of life's cycle endlessly; when we are worn out from watching the sunset of others, and we cannot possibly take in another with eyes open until the color is gone, we will find deliverance in the setting of our own suns, and be reborn in the hearts and minds of those who love us.

ABOUT THE AUTHOR

David Liscow, MD has been a practicing family physician in South Haven, Michigan since 1985. Inspired as an undergraduate at Duke University by the physician-writers, poet William Carlos William and Harvard psychiatrist Robert Coles, he has devoted his free moments when not tending to his busy practice or spending time with his family to research and writing. Dogs too have been an integral part of his life and family for three decades. During 2006, he lost both his father and his first puppy-to-grave dog. The final days of both experiences make up his second book, Diving into Sunsets. His first book, Symie's Story: Early Memories of an Old Jew Living in South Haven, was released in 2012.

Made in the USA
Lexington, KY
13 September 2017